Derek Young and **Gabriela Domicelj** became homeshare hosts accidentally. After living on their nine-acre property in the Blue Mountains, Australia, for two years, they moved to Singapore for work. They were reluctant to sell the property, so they asked friends to manage short-term rentals with the view to covering the property's costs. After a couple of years, they saw an opportunity to formalize the business and to drive both excellence and profit. Today, they are passionate supporters of the sharing economy, the growing Airbnb industry and delivering the 'perfect' guest experience.

After six years of building their homeshare business, they have learned the hard way what works and what doesn't, and what first-time homeshare hosts and those seeking to build their business need to know. When they first started managing their homeshare, they looked for practical 'how to' information and were surprised to find very little assistance. This book contains what they had hoped to find when they first started their journey of becoming homeshare hosts.

Derek has worked in wealth management for 30 years, providing fee-based financial advice to private clients, including as CEO of AXA ipac Asia in Hong Kong. He left the corporate world to pursue his own businesses – a wealth management company in Australia and consulting in Singapore. Gabriela has 25 years' experience in management consulting (with Accenture, Towers Watson and Aon), and five years' experience in film production, focusing on documentaries which tell the stories of private individuals and companies.

Derek and Gabriela have visited more than 50 countries as both business and leisure travellers, staying in backpacker accommodation as well as five-star hotels. They have both lived on four continents. They own two homeshare properties: an apartment in Sydney and Dantosa Blue Mountains Retreat (www.dantosa.com or Airbnb reference 1887805), which was named after their three children, whose middle names are Daniel, Tobias and Sacha.

Liana Cafolla interviewed Gabriela and Derek for this book and wrote some sections. She is a Hong Kong-based journalist, writer and editor who writes about business, people, trends and culture for the *South China Morning Post*, *Investor Relations* magazine, *LP Luxury Properties* magazine and other publications.

the home stay guide

Practical advice for Airbnb and homeshare hosts

GABRIELA DOMICELJ AND
DEREK YOUNG

ROBINSON

ROBINSON

First published in 2016 as *The Homeshare Journey*

First published in Great Britain in 2018 as *The Home Stay Guide* by Robinson

Authors' note

The opinions expressed in this book are those of the authors, who have done their best to check facts at the time of writing. However, the homeshare industry is so fast moving that the information, especially regarding online travel agencies, may become out of date. The advice presented in the book is general advice and is not specific to a single homeshare property or location. The authors cannot be held responsible for any business decisions made by readers; it may also be pertinent for homeshare hosts to obtain professional advice which is specific to their circumstances. It is assumed that individual homeshare owners have consulted local regulations to ensure that their business does not contravene any laws in their area.

A CIP catalogue record for this book is available from the British Library

ISBN: 978-1-47214-155-2

Typeset in New Caledonia LT by Hewer Text UK Ltd, Edinburgh
Printed and bound in Great Britain by CPI Group (UK), Croydon CR0 4YY

Papers used by Robinson are from well-managed forests and other responsible sources

MIX
Paper from
responsible sources
FSC® C104740
FSC
www.fsc.org

Robinson
An imprint of
Little, Brown Book Group
Carmelite House
50 Victoria Embankment
London EC4Y 0DZ

An Hachette UK Company
www.hachette.co.uk

www.littlebrown.co.uk

Contents

Foreword

For five years we have enjoyed living exclusively in homeshares around the world. Our vision was to live our daily lives in other people's homes for about the same amount of money we would have spent if we'd retired in Seattle. So far, so good!

However, without visionary companies like Airbnb and exemplary hosts like Derek and Gabriela, our fantastic retirement dream could not have come true. The homesharing industry is growing fast and people like us have more and more accommodation options beyond traditional hotels. We have been warmly welcomed into 160 different homes in 68 countries as valued guests and have been treated with great care and respect. And while our hosts often make it look easy, we know it goes well beyond a labour of love.

Managing a homesharing business comes with all the responsibilities of running a small hotel – only without the staff. That leaves you to be innkeeper, bookkeeper, head chef and bottle washer! From fluffing the pillows to filing the taxes, you need a wide range of skills and a keen eye on the bottom line to be successful.

That's why this book will become your most valued resource. Derek and Gabriela are seasoned international business and leisure travellers as well as acclaimed hosts, and they bring years of top-level experience in financial planning, business consulting and marketing alongside their passion for hosting to every page.

Whether you are just starting your endeavour or you're an experienced host looking to expand your operation, *The Home Stay Guide* is an easy-to-follow, step-by-step guide to creating a business that is mutually beneficial for you and your guests. From advertising your property and creating a unique interior to defining your guest experience, upgrading your financial management systems and managing your calendar, you'll find tips and tricks that will help you master the challenges and reap the rewards of the sharing economy. Guests like us will appreciate it if you 'go the extra mile'. If you adopt the recommendations made in this book, we are confident that over time your homesharing business will reap the rewards – and so will we!

In order to meet hosts who take joy in welcoming guests and have pride in offering all the comforts of home, we will continue our journey until we can no longer lift our luggage! Thank you for opening your homes to us and to travellers from around the world.

Debbie and Michael Campbell
The Senior Nomads
www.seniornomads.com

Introduction

Home stay, also known as homesharing, is a global phenomenon whereby ordinary people share their homes with strangers. As a homeshare host, you open the doors of your home, or offer your spare room or your sofa bed, to people who are looking for something more than just a hotel room. Your guests are looking for a sharing experience, a real insight into your home and your world, and the chance to take part in a new global community. Home stay is not a new concept, but recent technology has revolutionized its scale of operations, to the extent that homesharing is now disrupting the traditional hospitality industry. Homesharing is also opening up parts of the world where travellers would not traditionally stay.

Homesharing is a prime example of today's sharing economy: taking what is already there, and making the excess capacity available to those who need it. The sharing economy is developing through platforms provided by innovative companies like Airbnb and Uber, which are transforming economies and industries around the world and reshaping the way we view our homes, our possessions, and our interactions with strangers, as well as broadening our ideas about ownership and private property. And the sharing economy is becoming more and more creative, with people now sharing their storage space, boats, bicycles or local experiences, as well as their homes.

The speed and breadth of expansion in the sharing economy are unprecedented. In less than a decade, companies like Uber and Airbnb have grown in market value and size to outstrip many long-established players in the transportation and hospitality sectors. Powered by technology that allows effective distribution and online transactions through sophisticated platforms, the sharing economy is enabling everyday people to become entrepreneurs, to set up new businesses, to change careers and, to a far greater degree than ever before, to decide how and when they work.

The sharing economy is founded on one timeless principle of business and human relationships: trust. Participation in homesharing is the ultimate act of trust. Homeowners open up their properties to people from all over the world to stay in and to enjoy. Owners or hosts trust guests to take care of their property and prized possessions. Guests trust hosts to be 'open' when they arrive, and to deliver the property advertised and the guest experience promised by the attractive photos and detailed descriptions. Unlike global hotel brands such as Hyatt or Hilton, which build trust through their values and long experience, homesharing relies on trust represented by guest and host reviews, emerging accreditation labels such as Airbnb's Superhost status, and warranties provided by the technology platform providers – for example, Booking.com provides a back-up booking service in case a host cancels a guest's accommodation. The key to success in homesharing is creating a business that enables trust and delivers on its promises.

What drives you, as a homeshare host, to share your home with people from around the world whom you have never met? It may be to make the best use of unused or surplus space. Or perhaps you have a yearning to welcome people into your home and show off your neighbourhood. Maybe you want to take the plunge into starting a business. Or perhaps you own investment properties and would like to maximize your returns using an alternative to the long-term lease.

Whatever your reason, in the homesharing world, you are not alone. And if you are thinking about diving in, now is the time. The sharing economy is a global trend that is moving fast, and business is changing in ways that were inconceivable just ten years ago. It is a phenomenon that is very much a child of our times, a response, perhaps, to the search for ways to extract more from less. Whether it be environmental concerns about humans' impact on the environment, or the inequalities caused by the stresses of globalization, the sharing economy is one way that these imbalances can be redressed. By sharing what we have no need for, such as the space in our homes or holiday homes, we are collectively making better use of spare capacity. Those spare rooms which used to be occupied by your children are now available for travellers who need short-term accommodation. The availability of your children's bedrooms may mean that a hotel now needs to build one or two fewer rooms to satisfy the local market demand for accommodation.

This is not to say that homesharing is not a valid business opportunity. It is, and very much so. Airbnb's value is estimated at about US$30 billion (£23 billion); Uber, another sharing economy business, is estimated to be worth US$70 billion (£53 billion). Offshoots and copycats are springing up quickly around the world, multiplying the size of the sharing business. But it is not just the technology giants who are making money. You too can make a profit, and even a good living, from homesharing. We have seen our own revenue from hosting quadruple in five years. What's different about these businesses is the people behind them. As a homeshare host, you are both the face and the backbone of your business, the name your guests will know, the person they will talk about when telling their travel stories. You are the personality and brand behind your homeshare business. And your brand has global reach.

With the glory, of course, come the responsibilities. As a homeshare host, you and your offering will be compared and shared and reviewed around the world, many times. To succeed in this vibrant marketplace, you will need to offer a genuinely great experience, whatever the size and scale of your homeshare. Thanks to the reach of the online world, almost everyone can participate in the sharing economy, but only some will do it with excellence. This book, and our online sister service HomeShare Solutions, are designed to help you master the essentials of becoming a great homeshare host.

We learned these lessons ourselves the hard way, through trial and error. In 2012, we unintentionally stumbled into the homeshare business. We moved to Singapore for work reasons and had to decide what to do with Dantosa, our Australian home in the Blue Mountains. Friends offered to manage it as a homeshare and we decided that if the property could cover its costs, which was unlikely under a long-term rental arrangement, then turning it into a homeshare was a better option than selling it. After a year, and with minimal effort on our part, we were surprised to see that the homeshare property had delivered a profit. We began to take a greater interest in the business and became actively involved in sales and improving the guest experience, while remaining remote hosts. We next purchased a small city apartment in Sydney to run as a homeshare. Over the past few years, we have become intrigued by the business of homesharing and have fallen in love with homeshare hosting; we have grown and strengthened our business and achieved Superhost status on Airbnb, but the road has not been easy. We searched for a book like this when we started out, but could not find one.

Not all homeshares are successful. That is something we have learned first-hand from our own visits as guests to homeshares around the world. Some of our experiences were dreadful. When that happens, it is often not because the hosts don't care, but because they have not put enough thought and effort into turning their homeshare into something that meets the needs of guests. Doing this successfully requires a lot of preparatory work and planning – more than we realized ourselves when we set out as hosts. Running a homeshare operation is more complex than it first appears.

One area of complexity is regulatory; new regulations have varied greatly, in response to local community pressures. During the last couple of years we have been surprised by the extent of politicization around homesharing. Clearly there are hotel lobby groups fuelling some of the anti-homeshare activity, which is shrouded in a fear campaign: 'You won't know your neighbours any more', or 'What if the guests have noisy parties, or worse still, are indulging in illegal activities next door?', or 'Lock up your daughters, there are homeshare guests in the building.' During the Airbnb Open conference in Los Angeles in November 2016, there were well-organized and well-funded activists disrupting proceedings. Clearly the issue is complex, especially in crowded urban settings where there is a shortage of long-term rental accommodation available. The response from governments, both federal and local, has been varied. Some have embraced the concept, such as the governments of Seoul, Orlando and Amsterdam, actively promoting all aspects of the sharing economy. At the other extreme, there are local governments who have forbidden short homeshare visits, such as Barcelona, Berlin, Singapore and Vancouver. And in the middle ground are those local governments such as London and Sydney which are placing restrictions on the buildings permitted to provide homeshare accommodation and the proportion of time a property can be used for homeshare. This is new territory and it is likely that the rules of play will continue to evolve over the next few years. What is unprecedented, though, is the scale of disruption and the rapid pace of change. By June 2017 there were four million properties on Airbnb alone, a growth of over one million in a single year.

Our homeshare journey has been a steep learning curve, using common sense and above all, hard work – nothing can substitute for that. But it has also been filled with great people, new experiences and a sense of achievement. In the following pages, we share this experience with you, the good times and the bad, and provide detailed advice on how to get started and get ahead. This book is intended for people who are contemplating becoming homeshare hosts and for those who are already hosting but are keen to achieve excellence in their business. It will help you understand how to build trust into the reputation of your homeshare business, to see it thrive in a sustainable way.

The book is divided into three main sections. In 'Getting Started', we cover the basics of the hosting business

– marketing, sales, and the presentation of your property. The second section, 'Managing the Guest Experience', looks at the guest's experience from the moment of arrival to departure, handling transitions between guests, and dealing with reviews of your property. Finally, in 'The Business of Homeshare', we look at how to handle the numbers – financial management, reporting, and how to drive your business forward. Interspersed in the text, you will find comments and anecdotes from other experienced homeshare hosts. We interviewed a cross-section of hosts from around the world to seek the advice they could offer other hosts and to hear their stories. They come from 11 countries and are from both urban and rural settings, are hosts who share a bedroom in their own home as well as those who are absent, and they come from all walks of life. What they have in common is their passion for hosting. Their voices are included in this book to provide a breadth of information and opinions for our readers. We have also spoken with the most-travelled Airbnb guests, the Senior Nomads, about their experiences staying at 160 homeshares in 200 cities and 68 countries over the last four years.

Ours has not always been an easy journey, but it has been enjoyable and financially worthwhile; it is one that we highly recommend. After working in corporate roles for more than 25 years, in management consulting and wealth management respectively, we have been lured by the simplicity of the sharing economy and the benefits of owning our own business. With perseverance, curiosity and plenty of help from friends and professionals, we have learned a tremendous amount. This sharing of our experience and the lessons we have learned is designed to help you to accelerate your homeshare journey, and give you the confidence to participate in this twenty-first century economic phenomenon.

We hope you will enjoy your own journey as you set out on the homesharing path, and we wish you every success.

Gabriela Domicelj and Derek Young
August 2017

www.homesharesolutions.com

Part One
Getting Started

1
Marketing

Competent marketing of your homeshare property is essential to the success of your business. You may have the most wonderful homeshare property in town, but if nobody knows about it, your homeshare will remain a buried treasure. As with any product or service, marketing a homeshare is about telling the world exactly what you have to offer using the best possible words and pictures. This is the time when you take your carefully prepared accommodation and help it fly the nest, advertising it to compete against all the others.

> *We ran homeshare properties 25 years ago, and then it was difficult to market them. You were dependent on reviews from newspapers and word of mouth. All that has changed now; it's so easy to list a homeshare online today.*
> Yvonne, host from France and Australia

For hosts who are new to marketing, working out how to promote your property can seem daunting. Just take it step by step, and you will be able to build a successful online presence that will attract bookings. There are four main steps you will need to take. First, you need to stand back and assess your homeshare from the viewpoint of your prospective guests, and define your unique value proposition. Second, you need to identify your prospective guests so as to select the right online travel agency to reach them, and to set the tone of your communications. Third, you need to start to build a brand for your homeshare. Finally, you will need to create marketing content comprising text and pictures that will entice guests, and that also matches the requirements of the online travel agency where you will advertise your property. The following table depicts the four steps required to set up an optimum online presence.

How to market your property step by step

1. Know your homeshare
- Unique value proposition
- Listing description (property and host)

Messaging

2. Know your guest
- Target audience and purpose of visit
- Select appropriate online travel agency
- Set tone for communications

Communications

3. Build homeshare brand
- Name of homeshare
- Create identity (e.g. logo, website, colour scheme)

Imagery

4. Present sales message
- Refine sales message and listings
- Professional photography, hero shot
- Marketing materials

Package to sell

Marketing your homeshare is a challenging but satisfying journey that will enable you to get to know your property, your guests and your business in greater depth and build a stronger business.

THE UNIQUE VALUE PROPOSITION

The first step is to decide on your unique value proposition – a brief outline of what you are offering that is accurate, clear, descriptive, enticing and highlights what is unique about your property.

You need to be able to sum up the attractions of your home-share succinctly. Getting this right is vital, and it is worth spending time thinking about what makes your property stand out from the crowd, especially if it is similar to many other properties on the market. For example, to differentiate our Sydney apartment from dozens of other homeshares in the area, we highlight the flat's recent renovation and central location. Ask other people who are familiar with your property for their views on its best features – sometimes, another's eyes are more insightful.

> *You have to grab your audience's attention with the first photo on your listing. That photo needs to look warm and welcoming, not like a generic hotel room.*
>
> Brianna, host from Australia

Once you get it right, your unique value proposition will be invaluable for multiple purposes. You can use it to create interest in your property when meeting potential guests, or when introducing your property to an online travel agent. Printed on your business card, you can use part of it as a one-line marketing campaign. It can be the headline in any paid advertising you choose to do. If you are being interviewed about your property by the media, you can use it as an introductory statement to paint an immediate and clear picture of the property in the minds of readers and listeners. And it will be an effective aid to help focus your marketing materials and build consistency in your messaging.

Online travel agencies advise that the property description should not be too long, but it should include enough detail to enable readers to make an informed decision and give a real flavour of what is on offer. Visit the websites of similar properties for inspiration and for examples of description lengths. Make sure you write a description of yourself as a host; prospective guests are interested to know who owns the homeshare and want to get to know you personally.

KNOW YOUR CUSTOMER

Beyond the factual content, you will need to set a consistent tone for your marketing materials. This tone will depend on your target audience, and should also reflect your own personality. With marketing, you need to have a clear idea of who your audience is so that you can address them according to their interests and needs. When you are starting your homeshare business, it can be difficult to identify your target audience, but you can find plenty of helpful clues online. Start by reading the reviews for properties similar to your own to gauge the general guest profile for your property type. Look at your property, its price point and location through the eyes of potential guests and try to imagine what kind of people would like to stay there. A family with young children? An elderly couple? A group of friends? A business executive? Facilities in your area will help you define your target group more closely. Is your district famous for its hiking and climbing trails? A cultural oasis? A restaurant lover's delight? What about your property itself – is it designed for outdoor dining? Are there sports facilities on site? A vegetable garden that will attract food lovers? Consider all the attractions inside and around your property and the first shape of a target audience will begin to emerge. Over time, we have learned that Dantosa's major appeal is its exclusivity, which attracts groups who wish to spend time together in privacy, and we now focus our marketing on these guests.

Once bookings start coming in, you will have the opportunity to learn more about your guests and you can adjust the tone and content of your marketing materials accordingly. Remember, marketing is an imperfect and organic process. With every booking, you will build a clearer guest profile and understand better how to position your homeshare for future sales.

It is important to make sure that people's expectations and sense of privacy align with yours as a host; guests need to understand that this is a private home, not a hotel, and they should be respectful of the other residents (e.g. we updated our house rules to request no showers late at night).

Howard, host from Hong Kong

TIPS AND IDEAS
Finding your voice
Use the same tone in your marketing materials that you use for guest correspondence. As a guideline, consider the relationship your guest will have with you: if you are renting out a room in your home, use a more personal tone. If you're renting a large property as an absent host, use a more professional tone.

THE ONLINE TRAVEL AGENCY LANDSCAPE

The ever-growing number of online accommodation websites, booking services and online travel agents can make choosing a booking partner confusing for the new homeshare host. It is important to understand the choices available to you as a host and what their associated costs are. The industry is changing so fast that you must research your options at the time you are planning to list your homeshare property. If you are already a homeshare host, it makes business sense to stay up to date with new entrants to identify opportunities for listing your homeshare on other online travel agencies which target your preferred guests.

Today the key global online travel agencies are Airbnb, HomeAway (the parent company of VRBO), TripAdvisor and Booking.com. These online travel agencies have a strong reputation, a large number of homeshares available around the world, and offer a trusted service to both hosts and guests. There are other reputable and established online travel agencies which operate in certain geographies (for example OneFineStay, a United Kingdom-based site for luxury vacation homes) or cater for niche markets (for example Misterb&b, aimed at gay male travellers).

> *The key challenge in being a homeshare host is dealing with so many online travel agent portals, each with their own systems which are regularly updated without notice.*
>
> Derrick, host from Thailand

In the following pages we describe each of these online travel agencies and offer a comparison of their costs, features and services. Recommendations on how to select the most appropriate online travel agency are then made, based on the information currently available.

AIRBNB

Airbnb has a user-friendly platform and offers strong support for both hosts and guests. Their vision of 'belong anywhere' has been designed to resonate with global travellers, those who seek genuine experiences on their travels and do not perceive themselves to be tourists.

Airbnb's review process is more robust than those provided by other online travel agencies in that both host and guest are prompted to write reviews; Airbnb has developed a culture which encourages feedback and promotes homeshare excellence. The Airbnb Superhost designation identifies the best hosts, and potential guests can filter listings to select their homeshare using these criteria. Airbnb invests in its hosts' education and offers hosts opportunities to come together and share best practice with frequent local gatherings, as well as at their global Airbnb Open conference.

Airbnb charges its hosts 3% of the booking revenue, and guests pay Airbnb between 6% and 12%. They are one of the only online travel agencies to offer a host protection insurance fund which provides up to USD 1 million (around £758,000) in damages. One potential downside of Airbnb is that the host only receives contact details for the guest once the booking is confirmed, which does not allow for a phone conversation about any queries the potential guest may have. This can present a problem for hosts with complex properties, when potential guests would welcome a chat with the host prior to making a commitment to proceed.

Airbnb is growing exponentially and has over four million homes registered for homeshare, an increase of one million in less than one year. On any given night in 2016, a million people were staying in Airbnb homes in 65,000 cities around the world. As evidence of the impact of Airbnb on the home-sharing industry, the word 'Airbnb' is now making its way into the vernacular as both a verb and a noun meaning homeshare.

When you are starting out as a homeshare host, listing on Airbnb is a great place to start.

> *I have nothing but positive things to say about Airbnb. The platform is intuitive. It allows both hosts and guests to address varying circumstances (such as extending stays, updating pricing, issuing refunds, etc.).*
>
> Isaiah, host from the United States

HOMEAWAY AND VRBO

Expedia is a North American travel company that owns and operates international online travel brands, including those which cater to the vacation property and homeshare market. VRBO (Vacation Rentals by Owner) and HomeAway are Expedia's two well-known online travel agency brands, which also include sites such as Stayz, a well-supported website local to Australia and New Zealand. Depending on which brand and site is accessed, the host and guest experience varies. The VRBO tagline 'Escape the confines of a hotel' clearly positions their service in the homeshare space.

Expedia is seeking to harmonize the look and feel across its key sites, as well as its customer support and technology infra-structure. Focusing on VRBO and HomeAway, each site boasts more than two million properties. The cost for hosts and guests differ. There is the option for the host to take an annual subscription or pay per booking. Guests pay an additional fee of 4% to 9% per booking, depending on the aggregate book-ing rate charged. HomeAway has the same cost model. The other online travel agencies in the HomeAway family vary in fee model.

TRIPADVISOR

TripAdvisor is the world's largest travel company. Originating in the United States, it provides hotel and accommodation bookings, travel reservations and reviews of travel-related content, including interactive travel forums. TripAdvisor boasts more than 315 million members and over 500 million reviews and opinions of hotels, restaurants, attractions and other travel-related busi-nesses. It operates 25 travel brands including TripAdvisor, BookingBuddy, and in the homeshare sector, FlipKey and VacationHomeRentals.

11

The benefit of listing with TripAdvisor is the market reach and instant recognition that travellers have for the group brand. Challenges can occur when listing a property and managing a guest experience. Support for both hosts and guests is not easy to find, and the weak sense of community and mutual obligation between guest and host is evident. Like other large online travel agencies, the inability to connect with guests outside the TripAdvisor online messaging system can be frustrating. TripAdvisor is enhancing its online sites and services to improve the experience for both hosts and guests.

BOOKING.COM

Booking.com is another large global online player in the travel business, a travel fare aggregator and online travel agency for accommodation. One of the original major players in the online travel space, the site in the Netherlands has been owned and operated by the United States-based Priceline Group since 2005. The website lists over a million properties in 226 countries. The site was developed for booking hotel rooms, and the homeshare booking function feels like an added 'instant book' feature which does not allow host and potential guest to get to know each other prior to a booking being made.

From a homeshare perspective, its global reach and strong credentials makes Booking.com a site to consider for listing a homeshare property. However, the site's DNA is founded in hotel bookings. This means that the features required by hotel managers are also present for the humble host of a home-share property. The site is complicated for hosts to use, with features such as instant book, multiple rooms in the one property for separate guest groups, on-site parking options and real-time booking calendars. The fee model is similar to that used by the hotel industry, with a high commission rate of 15% charged to the host, although the cost to the guest is free.

One advantage Booking.com has is its access to the large and fast-growing Chinese travel market. In August 2012, Ctrip, a Chinese online travel company, and Booking.com formed a partnership with a commercial agreement which allows Booking.com hosts to advertise to the Chinese market. Homeshare hosts who have experience with online travel agencies and access to channel manager software (which helps manage multiple booking calendars in real time) may wish to consider Booking.com for their property.

LOCAL ONLINE TRAVEL AGENCIES

The concept of short-term vacation home rental is not new and many older websites have catered for this market for many years. Historically, they were developed with a geographic focus, similar to sites for estate agencies, so they offered vacationers a list of potential homes in a specific region. Many of these local online travel agencies are in fact the websites of local property managers who rent out a collection of properties in a certain place.

The online travel agency Stayz is an Australian site which was founded in 2001. It charges the host a high 10%, but the guest pays no booking fee. Stayz now has 40,000 homes available, but the website is not very easy to use. For complex homeshares, like Dantosa, potential guests can become confused by the quote given to them, which leads to many enquiries from travellers who cannot afford the total fees. Guest reviews on Stayz and other local online travel agencies are often not completed, making it more difficult to distinguish between homeshares to find one which truly offers a great guest experience.

TARGET ONLINE TRAVEL AGENCIES

The number of online travel agencies which target certain types of traveller is growing fast, as are their loyal client bases. These sites are curated and are typically easy to use and beautifully presented, aimed at attracting a specific potential guest category. Oasis is an online travel agency that began in 2009 in Buenos Aires; its 'home meets hotel' approach has now grown to cover a wider area than its original South American geography, and its homeshare properties are vetted for architectural design qualities to cater to the more visually discerning traveller. CouchSurfing is an online travel agency in San Francisco which connects hosts and guests around the world; it is aimed at young travellers on a budget. Take note though, as in researching the term couchsurfing it was found that in Europe, couch-surfing can be synonymous with sexsurfing, whereby hosts may assume that they can have sex with the guest in return for lodging.

Some niche online travel agencies target the luxury end of the market; these include OneFineStay (now owned by Accor Hotels) and Luxury Lodges of Australia. It is likely that the more successful luxury sites will build their own powerful and respected homeshare brands whereby their guests can travel the world staying at their branded homeshares in the way hotel guests do today.

There are also niche online travel agencies aimed at specific guest demographics. Wanderful, for example, states that they 'empower women to travel the world safely and confidently using a trusted and identity verified network of women across the globe'. Misterb&b 'envisions and helps create a world where gay men more easily travel and interact in the real world, fostering greater connections and strengthening the global gay community'. As a host, if you have a specific desire to host certain guests, it may be prudent to consider listing on a niche site that targets these groups.

COMPARING ONLINE TRAVEL AGENCIES

Each online travel agency has strengths and weaknesses and will appeal to different homeshare hosts and guests.

Before choosing an online travel agency, check the costs carefully. The costs of using different online travel agencies vary enormously. Some charge a fee to guests and some to hosts. These fees and the structure of charges can change over time, sometimes with dramatic consequences for hosts. For example, Stayz – owned by HomeAway and focused on the Australian vacation property market – used to charge hosts a flat fee of about US$12 (£9) per night, but then changed to charging a percentage of the total cost of the stay. For us, that meant costs escalated from US$24 (£18) to US$500 (£380) for some bookings at Dantosa, where rates are high for large groups in the peak season.

The following table will help you compare the fees charged by the key online travel agencies, information that is critical

15

when you are choosing the right online travel agency to promote your homeshare. The online travel agencies have different business models, charging either host, guest or both parties for their services.

Pricing Comparison

	Airbnb	HomeAway / VRBO Subscription	HomeAway / VRBO Pay per Booking	TripAdvisor	Booking.com
COST TO HOST					
Booking fee	3%	None	5%	3%	15%
Subscription fee	None	Annual fee	None	None	None
COST TO GUEST					
Service fee	6–12%	4–9%	4–9%	5–15%	None
Credit card fee	None	2.9%	2.9%	None	None

Source: websites of online travel agencies, August 2017

The next table compares the four key players relative to one another, and to local sites (for example Stayz in Australia or Oasis in South America), and target sites aimed at specific niche markets. The table is structured to compare features for the host, features for the guest and the reach provided by the online travel agency. Please note that this information is up to date at the time of publication, but is subject to change as competition between the online travel agencies increases.

Comparison of features of Online Travel Agencies

	Airbnb	VRBO / HomeAway	TripAdvisor	Booking.com	Local Sites	Target Sites
HOST FEATURES						
Cost to host and to guest	◐	◐	◐	○	○	
Payment (process and timing)	◐	●	◐	◐	●	
Ease of use	●	●	◐	○	○	●
Features for hosts	●	●	○	◐	○	●
Guest contact information available	○	◐	○	○	●	
Support	●	●	○	●	○	◐
Alignment with home-share industry	●	●	○	○	●	●
Listing flexibility	●	●	○	●	◐	●
Host protection fund	●	○	○	○	○	○
GUEST FEATURES						
Cost to guest	◐	◐	◐	●	◐	
Ease of use	●	●	○	◐	○	●
Presentation of information	●	●	◐	○	◐	●
Search facilities	●	◐	◐	◐	◐	
Guest review process	●	◐	◐	◐	◐	
Support	◐	◐	○	◐	◐	
Link to travel services	◐	○	●	●	◐	
REACH						
Geographic coverage	●	◐	●	●	○	◐
Reputation	●	●	●	●	◐	◐
Language support	●	●	◐	●	○	○
Number of listings	●	●	◐	●	◐	◐
Target business travellers	●	○	◐	●	○	◐

Note: The assessment of some criteria for target sites is blank, as it is too difficult to generalize.

● – very good

◐ – adequate

○ – weak

It is important to find out which online travel agency will promote your homeshare best. List your property with only one online travel agency when you are starting out. This will give you experience in managing sales, preparing your homeshare for guests, delivering a great guest experience and obtaining reviews; you will also avoid the potential calendar management problems associated with using multiple online travel agencies.

One way to identify your first online travel agency is to spend some time browsing different sites and opt for the one which has the greatest number of properties that are similar to your own. We recommend trying Airbnb first because it is well known, easy to use and has a strong community-based culture. Its global reach and multiple languages mean that you will be marketing your homeshare to people around the world.

BRAND – THE PERSONALITY OF YOUR HOMESHARE

Once you have mastered the basics of online marketing, you can start taking steps to turn your homeshare into a brand. Start by choosing a unique name for your property – this is a good marketing tool and one that is completely free. A name makes online searching easier for guests and helps to build a brand. Branding shows thought and care and builds an expectation of quality. Over time, it can add value and allow you to charge a premium. Your homeshare name can be used on photographs, and on emails and websites. We named our property Dantosa – a unique and personal name that comprises parts of the middle names of our three children – and we use the Dantosa logo for multiple purposes, including customized greeting and postcards, artworks for the house and as a design theme for soft furnishings in the property.

Unlike other online travel agencies, on Airbnb, the host, too, is part of the brand and is introduced through a photograph and a short biography that outlines his or her interests and background. We find this very effective in personalizing bookings and helping to build a relationship with guests.

SHOW, DON'T TELL

When it comes to marketing homeshare properties, a picture really is worth a thousand words. Photographs are the most important sales tool at your disposal, as they provide the only reliable insight into your property for guests. If you are investing in branding your property, it is essential to ensure that the photographs live up to the promise of your brand. Grainy, poorly composed shots will not do your property justice, and will probably lose you bookings. Hiring a professional photographer to take pictures of your property is worth the cost. Professionals have the wide-angle lenses and lighting equipment to present your property in literally the best possible light, inside and out.

Use realistic shots rather than ones that give misleading views from the property or show the neighbourhood as more appealing than it really is. If your photographs are misleading, guests will be disappointed as soon as they arrive, and that can be difficult for both the guests and the host to recover from. Instead, take the opportunity to be creative and show your personality. Is your garden full of beautiful flowers, or is there a friendly on-site gardener with a great smile? Take the shot.

Take advantage of Airbnb's offer to provide you with free professional photographs. The photographer who visited us gave good advice: photos must be realistic, well-lit and have no embellishment.

Romy, host from Hong Kong

Your set of photographs should cover all aspects of your property. Some online travel agencies impose a limit on the number of shots, but make sure that you have a sufficient number of photographs to represent the entire property. Include pictures that show a broad expanse of the rooms, rather than merely close-ups of small features. Give each shot a short, descriptive caption so guests know which room it is. If your property is in an apartment block, it is useful to include an exterior shot and one of the lobby to help your guests assess the quality of the building – and even to find it.

You must invest in a good photographer when you are starting out. Your pictures are your only selling point, so they must be appealing in order to translate into book-ings. Later your reviews, ratings and word-of-mouth refer-rals will form a basis of your marketing, but it is your photos that are the front-runner.

Sidharth, host from India

Increasingly, online travel agencies are introducing the option to upload video. It is likely that this will really take off as an important distinguishing feature of online travel agency sites. As the cost of technology storage continues to fall, video will become an increasingly important medium for marketing homeshares. Many homeshare websites run by hosts also provide video. The purpose is simple: to enable potential guests to gain a better feel for the space and amenities offered by the homeshare property. There is nothing quite like a private tour for enabling the guest to make a better-informed booking decision. In a market cluttered with tens of millions of photos of homeshare properties, video is a great way for your property to stand out from the crowd while subtly conveying a quality offering. Engaging a professional team that specializes in videoing homeshare properties is important for ensuring that the end product promotes your brand. A poorly produced video could damage your brand, so be careful who you hire.

TIPS AND IDEAS
The hero shot

Select one great photograph that says it all and lives up to the promise of your unique value proposition, and use this photograph widely. It may be a beautifully lit external shot of the whole property, or an evocative view of guests enjoying the property. Use this shot when only one picture can be used – for example, in a magazine ad or on a postcard, or for the homepage of your website.

TARGET YOUR MARKETING

If you have a budget for marketing, it will probably be limited when you start out. Focus your spending online. Start by building your own website, which should include at least a description of the property, photographs, an email address for enquiries, a booking calendar and if possible, a booking engine. With your own website, you avoid paying fees to online travel agencies for bookings. The content of your marketing materials should be honest, clear and set realistic expectations. Use simple language and frank rather than flowery descriptions that do justice to your property without encouraging your guests to have inflated expectations. If the apartment is on the fourth floor and there is no elevator, it is best to say so clearly on your website.

The website should include a layout of the space available, including bed sizes and configurations, so that guests can get a realistic picture of what space is available and where they will sleep. A clear layout also helps avoid repetitive email enquiries about what size beds are in which rooms. Upload the original house plans if possible, or use hand-drawn plans if these are not available.

For Dantosa, paid advertising pushes guests to the Dantosa website, where the conversion rate of enquiries to bookings is 40%, much higher than through other sources. Having more people visit your website also pushes you higher up the rankings via search engines, which can in turn lead to more visitors.

Most customers will come from online travel agencies or your own website, so consider spending some of your budget on search engine optimization to increase your visibility in search rankings. You can also take advantage of free marketing opportunities by setting up Facebook and Instagram accounts, where you can post messages about activities in your area or special events that may be of interest to holidaymakers. When starting out, it is important to use marketing vehicles with which you are familiar; do not feel you have to rush out and learn Facebook in order to be a homeshare host.

If your marketing budget is non-existent, don't despair. Most homeshare hosts never spend anything on marketing. By using

Airbnb and other sites to handle bookings and payments, you can easily set up shop without any marketing budget at all.

For more advanced marketing, the options are almost endless. It pays to think about who you want to target and then find out what kind of marketing can best reach them. Chapter 9, 'Driving Business', covers more advanced marketing for your homeshare business.

Summary

- Spend time working out your unique value proposition, and use it consistently in your marketing materials.

- Don't exaggerate your description of the property. Building up your guests' expectations only to disappoint them is to nobody's advantage.

- Clarity and accuracy are key to creating good marketing materials – and to avoiding reams of email questions.

- Set the tone of your communications in accordance with an understanding of your prospective guests, as well as your own personality.

- If you only spend money on one thing, make it professional photographs of the property. Select a hero shot, a picture which presents your property in its best light.

- For instant branding, give your property a name.

- Select your online travel agency carefully and start with just one.

2
Sales

Effective sales management for homeshares comprises three key elements, which are closely linked: setting market prices, persuading the prospective guest, and managing the online calendar. All have a hard-hitting effect on your sales. Set your prices too high relative to similar properties, and interest will likely flag. Set them too low, and you may be inundated with too many enquiries to handle. Fail to respond quickly and helpfully to enquiries, and your prospect will find alternative accommodation. And without effective tracking of actual and potential sales, your entire sales system is likely to fall apart. By following some simple guidelines and using the expert help available online, you will avoid potential calamities and build a healthy sales pipeline.

GETTING THE PRICING RIGHT

Setting prices for your homeshare involves considering variables such as competitor rates, season, days of the week, number of guests and length of stay. You will need to consider whether to charge per person or per room, and how much to charge during special events, such as a major conference taking place in your area. As a new homeshare host feeling your way in the business, you should aim to price your property at or just below the market average. You can find out what the market average is by checking the prices of similar properties in the same area as yours and in the same season. Another useful resource is hotel booking sites, where you can also gain an insight into pricing strategies by tracking how their rates change over a period of time. Doing this effectively will mean tracking their sites on a regular basis for a while until you become familiar with competitive pricing.

Step-by-step pricing

1. Do your research
- Competitor pricing (rates charged by similar homeshare in your area)
- Hotel pricing (rates charged by local hotels)

Research

2. Develop simple pricing rules
- Rate increase for peak periods (e.g. holidays)
- Extra charges for additional guests or services
- Add cleaning fee
- Set your security deposit

Pricing policy

3. Set a daily rate
- Determine minimum rate you are willing to receive
- Set daily rate or use demand pricing feature

Rates

Sophisticated hotels employ revenue management analysts to help them with pricing, and approach the task scientifically. The analyst's job is to maximize both occupancy and the average daily rate by analyzing past data and using a set of assumptions about dates, events and human behaviour. If you don't have access to these skills, a trial and error approach to pricing is a good way to start; you can always adjust your prices either up or down. Don't be afraid to increase your prices if demand is high. We set prices low when we started to market our Sydney apartment. As interest grew, he put the prices up. If you find that you are getting few enquiries about your property, it may be that you have set the price too high. One way to find out is by asking guests why they picked your property and consider adjusting prices according to their feedback.

I want mature sophisticated guests who would treat my home (artworks, possessions, kitchenware, etc.) like their own, so I charge a higher rate but offer a boutique hotel type service. I have white high-quality cotton bed linen, towels and beach towels, I leave welcome wine, chocolates and flowers, and provide Nespresso and sodastream machines, WiFi, Apple TV and toiletries. I also make sure that the house is spotlessly clean when they arrive, to justify my high rates.

Helen, host from Australia

When setting your prices, remember to include a cleaning fee in addition to the nightly accommodation charge. You should also request a security deposit from your guests, in case of damages.

DEMAND PRICING SYSTEMS

For less time-consuming price-setting, some online travel agents offer demand pricing systems to help hosts manage rates. Demand pricing is a market-based, automated pricing system where the price for accommodation fluctuates according to online demand in a specific location. A high number of searches for a certain type of accommodation or for accommodation on particular dates will result in increased prices, while slow periods and sluggish demand will result in lower prices. Depending on the online travel agency, hosts have the flexibility to set limits on the system within certain parameters while still benefiting from this time-saving feature. For example, Airbnb offers Smart Pricing™. This feature allows you to set your listing's price to adapt automatically to changes in demand. By switching on the feature, your property's daily prices adjust automatically within a minimum and maximum price range you have selected. Price adjustments are determined by a complex algorithm and are based on supply and demand for accommodation in your area on a specific date, your listing's features, location, amenities, booking history, and availability. Smart Pricing™ works on a rolling four-month period: when selected, Smart Pricing™ operates for the four months following the date you switch it on and then reverts to the standard rates you set previously. Smart Pricing™ can be particularly useful to new hosts who are unsure of what rates to charge their guests.

A clever aspect of this Airbnb feature is the ability it gives you to control both the ceiling and floor prices – particularly the floor price. This mean your accommodation is never offered at a rate lower than you are comfortable with and so you know, if you have done your sums, that you won't lose money. Provided you set a reasonable range for the ceiling and the floor, then your price is automatically adjusted according to demand for accommodation. This means less management at your end, as you don't need to keep such a watchful eye on events or happenings in your region that could cause accommodation rates to spike. You know that if your property is available and rates are surging, you will benefit from higher rates without lifting a finger.

Demand pricing systems are well understood and widely used by the hotel industry and are becoming par for the course on all kinds of online accommodation booking sites. Consumers are prepared for prices to change according to season and demand, and for different conditions of stay to apply during high-demand periods. In turn, hosts can choose to cut prices or reduce the minimum stay if bookings don't materialize as expected. At Dantosa, we set a four-night minimum stay during the Easter holiday period and we increase the price by 35–50%. If there is no interest, we drop the price a month before the holiday season to ensure that we receive a booking during that period. You can also choose to send last-minute offers to past guests if you have upcoming periods that have not yet been booked.

MANAGING ENQUIRIES

Successful hosts are quick to respond to all enquiries. Anyone involved in sales will agree that a prompt reply to an enquiry is a great start to a sale. It sends the message that you are professional, respectful, and willing to answer any questions that a prospective guest may have. If you know that you will be unavailable for a period of time, consider delegating the responsibility for answering enquiries to someone who is available. This might occur if you are on a long flight, at a work function, or travelling somewhere without internet access.

> *The more personal and welcoming the response to our enquiry, the more likely we'll book the rental even if a different property offers more of what we're looking for. A truly engaged host who's focused on a great guest experience makes up for a less-than-perfect listing every time.*
>
> *Senior Nomads*

The tone of your communication when responding to an enquiry should be friendly but competent. Take care to respond accurately, confirming availability for the dates requested, and answering specific questions in full. You may want to develop standard email templates to use in correspondence with guests at different stages of the sales process. These may vary from a placeholder message of 'Thank you for your enquiry. I am currently busy but will respond to you within two hours' to more detailed responses which include the answers to commonly asked questions, such as bed configurations or the maximum number of guests.

> *In 2012, I left full-time employment to travel for a couple of years. I initially wanted to rent out my apartment with a regular long-term tenancy, however there was very little interest. I then discovered Airbnb and thought I'd give it a go. With very low expectations, I happily received bookings immediately and we have been running the apartment as a homeshare ever since.*
>
> *Ricci, host from Hong Kong and Malaysia*

Several sites including Airbnb, Stayz, HomeAway, TripAdvisor and others offer a choice of template options for responding to guest enquiries. Some sites support automated response templates. Others allow you to choose the template that best responds to the guest's enquiry. When using templates, make sure to personalize them and check that you have the correct information; there is nothing worse than receiving an email that is clearly a poor cut-and-paste job and is perhaps addressed to someone else.

One trick we use is to use various email templates. Much of Dantosa's communication with prospective and confirmed guests is by email. Many email applications and some webmail systems allow you to save templates. Dantosa's email system is set up on Microsoft Outlook. We use Outlook's e-signature section to store our 15 different templates. Each template has a descriptive title, and when composing an email, we pull the appropriate template into the message body, complete with pictures and relevant hyperlinks. This is a very effective way to speed up the response process. And when you are dealing with several enquiries each day, finding a quick way to respond saves a lot of time.

All communications with prospective guests give you an opportunity to get to know them better. Take that opportunity. Try to understand the purpose of their visit and what factors are critical for them in deciding where they stay – such as cost, location or permission to bring their pet. Communication, whether by email, text, WhatsApp or a phone call, also allows you to form an impression of the person enquiring, which will help you decide whether your homeshare will meet their needs and if they will be a desirable guest.

Dantosa has a strict rule that it is not to be used as a party house. If guests are planning to hold an event such as a BBQ with invited visitors, they need to inform us of their plans first. We had a guest who wanted to play loud music until the early hours of the morning. Dantosa has neighbours and the noise carries. After asking the enquirer some questions and explaining the importance of noise control and respecting the neighbours, it became clear that the enquirer would not be suitable for Dantosa. We politely suggested that the enquirer search for an alternative venue where music was allowed without restrictions.

TIPS AND IDEAS
Tracking sales enquiries

Keep a record of all enquiries – a sales pipeline. This should include the name of the prospect, the date of enquiry, their contact details, the source of the enquiry and its status. If an enquiry is unsuccessful, try to find out the reason that the person did not proceed with the booking. These records will help you to forecast future sales and will give you insights into changes you may need to make to your sales approach, such as adjusting pricing or improving response times. Your sales pipeline and your booking schedule will also influence your marketing by helping you to pinpoint which type of guests best suit your property and how to target them.

WHEN IS A BOOKING NOT A BOOKING?

An enquiry about making a reservation is not to be confused with a reservation that has been confirmed by the payment of a booking deposit. Until the booking deposit – or payment in full, if that is your policy – has been received, then no booking has been made and as a host, you should not make any changes to your availability calendar.

We learned this lesson the hard way in the early days. A potential customer asked us to block out certain dates while he consulted the rest of his party. We obliged and marked the dates as booked. However, the confirmation never materialized and we lost several days' worth of sales opportunities, ending up with no booking for those dates. Nowadays, we refuse requests for informal reservations and operate on the principle of 'first come, first served'.

CALENDAR MANAGEMENT

It may seem like an easy task – after all, who doesn't have to maintain a calendar of some sort in their daily life? But when it comes to running an online homeshare business, calendar management can become tricky. So before you sign your property up to every online travel agency you can find, take some time to consider what calendar management entails.

Consider some of the parameters you will need to set and the safeguards that you need to have in place before you start filling in details of your property's availability online. Some of these are more complex than they may at first seem and you may need to do some research to understand the guidelines and terms of use of each website. For instance, should you set availability by counting the number of nights people stay, or by counting the number of days the property will be occupied? How do you set check-in and check-out times? And what if you forget to update the online calendar and find yourself with confirmed bookings for the same dates on more than one online travel agency?

I suppose the worst thing about hosting is the adminis-tration – not so much tracking guests, or gathering their passport information for the tourism authority, coordinat-ing transportation, etc. – but in managing availability displayed on the various booking sites. I now know that I must immediately update my other calendars if I secure a guest from another site – otherwise a guest can book and then it is up to me to find them an equivalent booking!

Tom, host from Croatia and Sweden

Before getting started, be realistic about how much time you can devote to running your homeshare business. Remember that if your property is listed on multiple websites, you will need to be prepared to monitor and update multiple calendars every time you take a new booking. If you are new to the rental business, or have only a limited amount of time to devote to managing your homeshare business, you may want to start small by choosing just one site to list on and build your prop-erty's exposure as you come to understand the time and management involved.

Maintaining calendars on multiple sites also means multiple enquiry points from prospective guests. You will need to ensure that you can read and respond to all the different message channels that you have enabled. These may include messages sent through the various websites, emails to one or several email addresses, text messages, push messages and phone messages. To manage these effectively, you will need to ensure that you have access to WiFi at all times and to mobile roam-ing services when you are travelling. If that sounds like too much commitment, don't opt for 'instant bookings' (see box page 35). If you do, you could find yourself with too much work to handle, not to mention impatient and frustrated potential guests. Take on only what you can realistically manage.

TIPS AND IDEAS
Instant bookings

Online travel agencies such as Booking.com and Airbnb offer an instant book facility. This means that when a guest selects dates and guest numbers for a specific property, they can book it immediately without the need for engaging in an enquiry process with the host, just as on an online hotel reservation site. This feature offers several major advantages. From the guest's perspective, it saves time and secures their reservation immediately. Guests may spend significant time reviewing different properties, their amenities, features, location and price. After making a decision, they are often ready to book straight away. The instant book feature also suits guests who need to make a last-minute booking quickly.

From the host's viewpoint, instant book facilities save time – a lot of time. We offer several booking options at Dantosa on instant book. Again, like the guest, we do not need to respond to enquiries. The booking is made and the first time we communicate with the guest is to thank them for their reservation and make arrangements for their stay. The timesaving means more time is available to focus on other areas of the business – the guest experience, marketing or operations.

Don't set yourself up for failure. If you use an instant book facility, be sure you can deliver the homeshare to guests at the times indicated as available on your calendar.

I had guests staying and they had requested a late check-out. But in the meantime, other guests had booked using Airbnb's instant book. That hadn't happened to me before. I had made plans with friends, but when I saw the new booking I realized that the new guests were arriving within the hour. I had to scrap my plans, and go and clean the house.

James, host from Australia

HOW MANY CALENDARS?

Take heart. With realistic expectations and clear-headed planning, most calendar management problems are in fact very straightforward. It may also be reassuring to know that managing a calendar does not require special skills or computer programming knowledge.

It is not technically demanding. In fact, it is very user-friendly. There is also an online community that can help, and you can refer to blogs to find answers to your calendar questions.

For years, hotels have faced the same challenge of managing different online calendars. Software packages designed for the hotel industry can help align calendars automatically. Called 'channel managers', these systems centralize booking management and update external online calendars in real time. Similar packages exist for homeshare hosts, but you need to pay to use them and they vary in their ability to meet the needs of homeshare hosts. Airbnb has joined forces with Live Rez, an online calendar management platform designed for homeshares (www.liverez.com). If you opt to use this service, you will be able to centralize your homeshare calendar management. If you prefer to go it alone, you will need to update each website's calendar individually. It may be wise to list on only one booking site until you have got the hang of managing a booking calendar. Once you progress to more than one online calendar, setting up a central or master calendar can be a great way to help ensure all your calendars are aligned. This master calendar could be maintained as a spreadsheet. Remember that to make it work effectively, you will have to ensure that the master calendar is always kept up to date.

> *It is critical to align your calendars across the online travel agent platforms that you use. We do it manually as we've found the technology for calendar syncing available today to be disastrous.*
>
> Yvonne, host from France and Australia

ACCURACY AND TIMING

Accuracy in your calendar availability is key. Block out the wrong dates and you have blocked off potential sales. Forget to block out dates and you leave yourself open to the dreaded double booking.

Also block off dates when your property is not available for reasons other than rentals. These may include times when you need to schedule maintenance or in-depth cleaning, dates when friends or family members will be using the property, or when you want to use it yourself.

> *Homeshare provides us with flexibility, unlike long-term letting. Now we can invite our extended family to stay in between paying guests.*
>
> Megan, host from the United States

Remember, if you select 'instant bookings', you need to be able to ensure that the property is permanently in a rentable condition.

Pay special attention to how each website counts booking days, because they can differ markedly. For example, if a guest books a visit of Friday, Saturday and Sunday nights, Booking.com will count that as three nights, but other sites may count it as four days, because the guest will still be in the property for part of Monday. If you have another guest checking in on Monday morning, you could be in trouble unless you are able to arrange for a tight transition in between the check-in and check-out times.

Setting sensible check-in and check-out times is crucial. You need to ensure guests are aware of these times, and that you have enough time to arrange for cleaning and preparation of the home before the next guest arrives.

THE IMPORTANCE OF SPEED

An up-to-date calendar requires a focused approach and a commitment to keeping your calendar updated. This is a non-negotiable commitment if you want to rent out your homeshare online, and you will find there are multiple benefits. Having an up-to-date calendar means you can make quick decisions on bookings and confirm faster, resulting in more bookings and more satisfied customers. Remember, guests will likely have emailed several hosts with the same booking enquiry, and if you are the first to respond, you are more likely to get the booking.

Maintaining a mindset of timeliness and fast responses is essential. The quicker you answer an enquiry, the more likely you are to make a sale. Nowadays, customers expect a response within an hour.

As well as securing more bookings, quick responses will gain you better status on some websites. For example, being designated an Airbnb 'Superhost' partly depends on the speed of your responses. Customers often post positive comments on the speed of response from a host, adding to your attractiveness and thus encouraging more bookings.

Some hosts choose not to keep their calendars up to date in the belief that they will get more enquiries. That may be true, but you will end up wasting a lot of time answering individual queries about availability. It is important to remember that most people who contact you are planning a holiday or business travel, and in the vast majority of cases, guests are not flexible with their dates. It is also worth bearing in mind that guests are not browsing for a hobby – they are likely to be time-poor and do want to make a booking. They don't want to waste time on sending enquiries if the property is not available for their required dates.

DEALING WITH CANCELLATIONS

Different online travel agencies have different cancellation policies and some allow the host to select the severity or leniency of their policy. On Airbnb, the host can choose from three standardized cancellation policies – Flexible, Moderate and Strict. In addition, a Super Strict policy is available to selected hosts, along with another policy designed for long-term bookings. Overall, cancellations are relatively rare because of the community spirit that the Airbnb site encourages. Dantosa has had only three cancellations out of approximately 400 bookings over six years.

On the Dantosa website, we maintain a strict policy on cancellations, and we recommend this policy to other hosts. If a booking is cancelled, no refund of the deposit is made to the guest. The reason for this is that homeshares are fundamentally different from hotels, where deposits are typically refunded. Unlike a hotel, a homeshare can only sell each night once – there is no alternative room or property from which to earn income, so hosts must be more careful about protecting their income. In addition, while hotels are often booked at the last minute, homeshares such as Dantosa usually operate on a two-month booking timeline, making last-minute bookings very unlikely.

THE DREADED DOUBLE BOOKING

If two sets of guests are confirmed for the same dates, it is a signal that something in your calendar management system has gone seriously wrong. You will need to go carefully back through all the steps in each of the booking processes to find out what happened, and take action to ensure that it cannot happen again. But first, you need to resolve the immediate problem: informing one set of guests that their confirmed booking is not going to happen and, if possible, helping them find alternative accommodation.

We speak from experience when we say that this is a situation best handled with speed, tact and help from your online booking partners. One time, two bookings were confirmed for our homeshare on different websites by two separate groups, for the same dates, and we had to find a solution.

The first booking came in from an online site with no 'instant book' facility. We responded to the booking and confirmed it. But we forgot to adjust the availability on the Booking.com calendar, where the property was also listed and which does have an 'instant book' service. A second booking came through that site for dates that overlapped with the first booking, and the booking was instantly confirmed by Booking.com. At the time, Booking.com only notified hosts of bookings via text message. As luck would have it, we were on a flight at the time and missed the message. We only saw it a few days before the two bookings were due to start. The timing could not have been worse. It was Christmas, and Booking.com had already charged the credit card.

Adopting the mindset of a hotel concierge, we decided that we simply had to resolve the problem for that group. We spoke to the clients by phone, apologizing and explaining the problem – all in broken English, as they were not native English speakers. We then spoke to Booking.com and explained what had happened. Booking.com were able to speak to the clients through a translator, and together we worked out a solution and found the guests alternative accommodation. We were charged a US$100 penalty by Booking.com to cover their administration costs. But the real cost was in the time it took us to resolve the situation and our reputation as homeshare hosts.

This experience helped us define some guiding rules for avoiding similar situations in the future. The golden rule is to honour the booking of whichever client booked first – and if that means losing out on a booking that is longer or more lucrative, that's just tough luck. We recommend getting in touch with the client immediately by phone to let them know there has been a mistake. In some cases, you may find that the client is able to change their dates, but that is not typical, especially with group bookings.

> *I once had a confirmed booking and forgot to update the availability on another site, which resulted in a double booking for the same dates. I then had to find the second guests another place to stay, which happened to be over the New Year period, which was tough to do.*
>
> Sidharth, host from India

It is essential to understand the rules of engagement of each online travel agency, as they may all be different, and to work out how you are going to manage the different communication and confirmation channels. In six years of hosting, we have had just two double bookings. Those were enough to prove to us the need to be organized when dealing with calendar management.

Four key sales principles

1. *The golden rule is be responsive.* Reply as quickly as possible to all enquiries. Remember, the early bird catches the worm.

2. *Track your enquiries.* Create a 'sales pipeline' spreadsheet especially for the purpose, including guest name, dates of interest, and contact details if these are available. This data will help you track the interest in your property, identify which online travel agency the potential guest came through, and chase enquiries from whom you have not heard back. We believe that most hosts don't track this information. If you plan to build your homeshare into a profitable business, this information will help achieve your goal.

3. *Build a sense of urgency into your online communication.* Encourage enquirers to make a definite booking decision quickly. Even a 'no' answer can provide you with valuable insights if you can find out why they chose not to proceed with the booking.

4. *Engage your guests personally.* If they are booking for a special occasion, acknowledge this by email and

consider providing a gift. As well as being a good sales tactic, getting to know your guests will help to establish a relationship and build rapport.

Thanks to Derek, who has 30 years of sales management experience, we have proved the effectiveness of personal engagement through sales figures: when we tried outsourcing sales, Dantosa had an enquiry-to-sales conversion rate of 2–3%, but when we took over the sales personally, the rate surged to 30–40%.

Summary

- Decide how much time you can really devote to your homeshare business.

- Study the booking rules of each online travel agency you plan to use and stay up to date with changes to their sites.

- Keep the number of online travel agencies you use to a minimum when you are starting out as a host.

- If you have more than one source of enquiry, commit to keeping all calendars up to date.

- Consider using an online pricing calculator to set your nightly rate.

- Get organized by maintaining a master calendar.

- If problems arise, step in quickly to resolve them.

3

Presentation of Your Homeshare Property

The presentation of your property is not only a statement of your personality, but the key to a strong business. First impressions count, and how your property looks when guests arrive will play a large part in getting their stay off to a great start.

> This is all about hospitality. If you walked into a Hilton hotel and there were items strewn about the lobby, dust on the furniture, unwashed dishes on the counter, etc., what would you think? Would you want to stay there again? Probably not.
>
> Isaiah, host from the United States

Before you start renting out your property, you need to take an objective survey of the interior and see it from a guest's perspective. You also need to plan and stock up on the furniture, equipment and supplies you will provide for your guests and ensure that the property is safe.

Remember, some of the best – and most memorable – features of your homeshare's presentation cost nothing or next to nothing. These include ensuring the property is well-aired before guests arrive, turning on a welcoming light over the front door, arranging some fresh flowers and leaving a welcome note.

SETTING THE STAGE

Opinions abound about interior design for homeshare accommodation. This mainly depends on your personal taste and budget. One school of thought suggests decorating according to a particular theme such as a pirate's cave, a Disney movie, or a blue and white Greek beach house. This will make your homeshare distinctive and will appeal to some, though not all, potential guests. Before you decide on a design scheme, consider the likely taste of potential homeshare guests and the practicalities of maintaining your décor. The key is to find a balance between a spare interior that could look too sterile and uninviting and décor that is too overwhelming. To create a streamlined effect, choose two or three colours, and use these as your core palette throughout the property. We believe that the interior of your homeshare should be simple, fresh and clean, rather than being a specific feature in itself. This will maximize the number of people interested in your homeshare and make maintenance easier.

Paint walls in neutral tones and repaint them regularly. Take special care when deciding which pictures and ornaments to display. Avoid imagery that could cause offence, for example religious or humorous art works.

Ensure that the lighting in your homeshare is adequate and that bulbs are working. Remember that your guests have never been to your place before and at night they need to be able to see their way around the entire property, including the outside areas.

> *Sometimes you need to let go of the 'perfection instinct'. There is a grey area between providing what most people want and delivering the world. It's getting that balance right which is the art to homeshare hosting.*
>
> Megan, host from United States

COLOURFUL CLUTTER V. CLEAN AND SIMPLE

Guests like to move into a space that has been prepared to host them and their belongings comfortably, rather than a room filled with other people's things. It is best to remove all your personal belongings, ornaments and anything else that is not essential for the comfort of your guests. They may be treasures to you, but they will be clutter to your guests. Err on the side of less is more: if you are unsure whether or not to keep an item on display, remove it.

> *You need to really put effort into decluttering your home, making adequate space in wardrobes and bathrooms for guest belongings and having a super clean home.*
>
> Helen, host from Australia

FURNISHING YOUR HOMESHARE

When preparing your property to become a homeshare, you must review your furniture. If the property is currently unfurnished, then you need to invest in appropriate furniture. Buy new, sturdy furniture in a style that will not date quickly.

47

If your property is already furnished, this is the time to be ruthless. Remove any unnecessary furniture from each room and examine all items of furniture to see whether they need to be replaced or repaired. An old chest of drawers may seem charming to you as a family heirloom, but a guest may view it as anachronistic and ready for the bonfire. If you find it difficult to be objective, ask for the frank advice of a friend or relative: what should stay, what should go and what needs to be replaced?

> My place is deliberately not fancy because I want people to feel at home and comfortable. I have not bought new furniture because I want my guests to think it's okay to put their feet up on the sofa, like they might do in their own home.
>
> Ingrid, host from the United States

Focus on providing the most important elements in each room. A good night's sleep is what your guests will remember most. Take a leaf from the hotel industry, which worked this out years ago. Invest in high-quality beds, comfortable mattresses and pillows, and good-quality linen. Remember, many of your guests are used to staying in hotels. Aside from a great bed, your homeshare bedrooms need bedside tables, wardrobe hanging space and a full-length mirror. After a few years in operation and at the request of guests, we also decided to provide luggage racks in each bedroom.

Bathrooms should be functional and visibly clean. They are the last place seen at night and the first place encountered in the morning, so ensure that they are sparkly clean when the guests arrive. Provide a sufficient quantity of high-quality towels for your guests, and put spare toilet paper in each bathroom.

Furniture in the living areas of the property should suit the number of guests who will be staying. If your property is advertised as being suitable for up to six people, then ensure that your dining table has at least six chairs and that the living area provides enough seating.

TIPS AND IDEAS
Setting the lux level

The range of supplies you provide should match the luxury level of the accommodation. For example, at Dantosa Blue Mountains Resort, guests are welcomed with a bowl of fruit and a hamper of local produce, including muesli, chocolates, tea, cookies and honey, and the kitchen is equipped with extras, such as a spice rack. A luxury local brand of liquid soap, shampoo, conditioner and hand lotion is provided in bathrooms to pamper guests and to promote another local business. In our Sydney apartment, however, only the basic bathroom and cooking ingredients are supplied.

SUPPLIES AND SPECIAL TOUCHES

Small touches such as providing good quality soap in the bathroom can help build your brand and provide an easy way for your guests to equate your homeshare with quality. Decide on a policy for providing supplies. First, consider each room in the property and what supplies are required. Then decide what quality to provide. It is best to avoid the cheapest products

– remember, guests will be using them frequently and will notice the quality. Some homeshare hosts seek to emulate a four-star hotel experience for their guests. They provide high-quality linen, soap and shampoo. Others include bathrobes and hand lotions. At the other end of the scale, some hosts offer an inexpensive, bare-bones experience and do not provide any supplies for their guests other than toilet paper. The cost of supplies can add up quickly and it is important to ensure that replacement costs are factored into your overall pricing.

If your guests have access to a kitchen, we recommend providing basic cooking supplies such as olive oil, salt, sugar, coffee and tea. Provide fresh milk in the refrigerator and sponges, cloths and washing-up detergent at the sink. If you have a washing machine which guests can access, consider providing washing powder for their use.

> *Make sure that your private areas are locked up. One time a guest arrived when I was not there and they went upstairs into my living area, as opposed to the downstairs homesharing apartment. This caused great confusion as it did not look ready for their visit.*
>
> Ingrid, host from the United States

GETTING EQUIPPED

Just as you need to plan what supplies to provide for guests, you also need to decide what equipment will be available. You may want to provide as much equipment as possible for your guests' comfort, but bear in mind that equipment breaks down and will require maintenance, which will cost you time and money as well as inconveniencing your guests.

You need to pay attention to detail when you present your property. I want to be able to open the bathroom drawer and see that the hairdryer has been cleaned and its cord is recoiled neatly.

Brianna, host from Australia

At a minimum, you will need to provide the following:
- a television with cable channels and/or internet access to Netflix, Apple TV, etc.
- a hair dryer in each bathroom
- toaster, kettle, pots and pans in the kitchen, and enough crockery, cutlery and glasses for the maximum number of guests.

As a host, we recommend that you pack your own suitcase and stay in your own homeshare for a few nights. Pretend you're the guest, and don't bring anything you wouldn't pack for an enjoyable weekend away.

Senior Nomads

Consider whether your guests may have any special requirements. Even if these have not been specifically requested, guests will appreciate your thoughtfulness in providing them. Based on guest feedback, we now provide guests at Dantosa Blue Mountains Retreat with a portable cot and high chair for families with babies and toddlers, high-quality coffee machines, and a wok, chopsticks and a rice cooker to appeal to guests from Asia.

Provide new equipment, maintain it well, and be prepared to replace it once it starts to look old. Guests appreciate decent crockery and glasses, and new sets are generally not expensive. When buying equipment for your property, consider buying additional items as spares to replace breakages. This will avoid the difficulty of finding matching items later. At Dantosa, for some reason, bedside lights are the one item which seem to break regularly, so we keep a supply of spares in stock.

> *It is the detail that counts. Many of our guests have complimented us on providing zip-lock sandwich bags, which they use to put their mobile phones in when they go to the beach.*
>
> Brianna, host from Australia

GUEST SERVICES

Many guests say that the most important service is reliable WiFi access. Negative reviews left by guests often relate to problems with internet connectivity. If your property is hosting business guests, reliable WiFi and internet are paramount.

Providing reliable WiFi sounds simple, but breakdowns can occur and it is vital to ensure that you have a back-up plan if problems arise with your internet access. The Dantosa properties have fixed-line broadband with WiFi area networks. A cellular broadband set box acts as a back-up, so that if the fibre-optic cable fails for any reason, guests can resort to the hotspot provided by the cellular box. Depending on your carrier, the cellular option is likely to be more expensive and requires some set-up time. Alternatively, hosts could make available a USB dongle for guest use. It is worth the effort: guests will thank you for the back-up and will remember you went the extra mile when struck by an internet crisis.

You may choose to include the speed of your WiFi in your homeshare listing so guests know what to anticipate (see speedtest.net). You can also inform guests of the quality of mobile phone coverage at your homeshare, including the reception available by mobile phone provider.

TIPS AND IDEAS
Are you business ready?
Airbnb has set up a classification of properties which are deemed 'business ready'. To appeal to business travellers, ensure that your wireless internet is reliable and that your property can be accessed 24 hours a day. The property also needs to be smoke and pet free, with a laptop-friendly workspace, a smoke detector, an iron, coat hangers, hair dryer and basic essentials – toilet paper, shampoo, clean towels and fresh linen.

Depending on the nature of your homeshare and your guests, consider offering guests the option of having local businesses come to your homeshare to provide their services to your guests. For example, at Dantosa Blue Mountains Resort, guests are offered a choice of local chefs who can come and cater for them, massage therapists, and winemakers who conduct wine tastings. Only recommend local service providers whose services you have experienced and if you have confidence in their reliability and quality. You can consider charging these business suppliers a referral fee to supplement your income.

SAFETY AND SECURITY

It is essential to ensure that your guests feel, and are, safe when staying at your homeshare. This means that you have clearly communicated emergency procedures such as the location of the fire exit and meeting place, and provided a list of emergency numbers and contacts. You also need to ensure that a full set of safety equipment is in place. Provide a fire extinguisher and fire blanket in the kitchen, as well as a first-aid kit, and instal smoke detectors in the property.

Explain to guests how to lock up and access the property, and give them any relevant information about safety in your neighbourhood. Keep spare sets of keys to the property in case your guests forget to return them, or accidentally lock them inside the property. Many hosts now prefer to use digital locks instead of keys to avoid the complications of lost keys.

Consider installing digital locks to allow guests access to your property via a code. Many types of locks are available, with varying degrees of complexity and functionality. The benefit of a digital lock is that guests can access the property without the need for the host to be there in person. Also, security codes can be changed between guests and some enable online access to the lock's codes. This allows a host to set a code for each group of guests, for a defined period. After check-out, the code can be changed for the next visitor.

I have installed a key safe and give guests a code so they can arrive or depart at any time, without needing to have someone available to meet them.

Helen, host from Australia

MANAGING RISK

As a homeshare host, you should run a responsible business. This means ensuring that you have adequate insurance coverage not only for the contents and property, but also for your guests and for accidents on the property. It is important to seek professional advice to find the appropriate coverage for your property. This will be determined in part by the nature of your property. For example, the Dantosa Blue Mountains Retreat is situated close to a national park and the risk of wild fires is one factor that needs to be covered by the insurance policy. As the owners of a large property that is often hired by groups, we hired an insurance assessor to audit the risk and provide a tailor-made insurance policy.

As the growth of the homeshare industry gains momentum, some companies have begun offering purpose-designed insurance for short-term accommodation. This insurance allows you to purchase cover for the period of your guest's booking, and is intended to supplement standard home contents insurance. Claims for personal accidents, public liability and malicious or accidental damage are covered. For example, the Sharecover policy, available in Australia (share-cover.com), is underwritten by IAG and offers top-up cover for the additional risks associated with homeshare hosting.

TIPS AND IDEAS
Leave it, and be willing to lose it
A word of advice for hosts who are letting out an entire property: be willing to lose what is there. Don't leave valuables or irreplaceable objects in the homeshare

because unlikely breakages and thefts do happen. Many hosts leave favourite items for guests to enjoy only to find some time later that they have been broken. In the early years of Dantosa's listing, the family's electronic piano was kept in the property for guests to enjoy. Many guests had sing-songs around the piano and some left reviews commenting on how much they enjoyed the experience. Then one day a guest spilt a drink over the piano, and it no longer functioned. As the discovery of the 'deceased' piano only occurred many guest groups later, the damage could not be recovered. Experience was the only benefactor.

Some online travel agencies offer varying degrees of cover in select countries. A standout is Airbnb, whose Host Protection Insurance programme provides primary liability coverage for up to US$1 million in the event of third-party claims of bodily injury or property damage. The programme may also cover claims if a guest damages the property, and includes claims filed by a landlord against a host. We experienced the benefits of this policy first-hand when expensive matting in one of the bedrooms was damaged during a guest's stay. Airbnb's programme paid for the replacement of the floor coverings.

To minimize the number of accidents or breakages in your property, provide clear terms and conditions and have your guests confirm their acceptance of these in advance of their stay. Set clear expectations, such as 'this is not a party house', and explain the conditions under which you may need to retain their security deposit, such as when extensive cleaning is required or if an expensive item has been broken.

Our friends think we are crazy leaving our home to strangers, especially when we leave our artwork and favourite books in the apartment. But we have only had one bad experience with disrespectful guests in all the years we have been hosts.

Yvonne, host from France and Australia

The good news is that guests on the whole are very careful and do abide by the rules you set out for them. At Dantosa, there have been very few incidents of breakage and no thefts to date. Guests seem to recognize that they are staying in someone else's home and are considerate during their visits.

Summary

- Keep the décor simple to appeal to as many guests as possible.

- Declutter ruthlessly, including getting rid of unnecessary furniture.

- Set a policy for your supplies and factor in the cost.

- Be intentional about the quality of linen, towels, toiletries and guest gifts; if you want to offer a five-star experience, then provide high-quality accessories.

- Insure your property fully and provide safety equipment.

Part Two
Managing the Guest Experience

4

The Guest Experience

The guest experience is paramount. As a homeshare host, what is it that you want your guests to remember after they leave? What are the best features of your homeshare that you want to ensure that your guests experience? What supplies and decorations will you provide for your guests? While there is no perfect one-size-fits-all solution, your guest experience should include the following elements: a warm welcome, the sense of being looked after during the stay, and a friendly departure.

> *We've been fortunate to stay in some great homes. The homeshares that stand out usually have more to do with the hosts and how they made our experience memorable by sharing their culture and their hospitality, than the physical place or even the location.*
>
> Senior Nomads

First impressions count and it is important that your guests feel welcomed, albeit often by a remote host, when they arrive at your homeshare. They should also feel safe and 'looked after' during their visit, even if that is by such simple means as having a welcome book that gives information and a phone number to call if they have questions. Your guests' check-out should be equally straightforward and a good experience,

Dantosa guest communications process

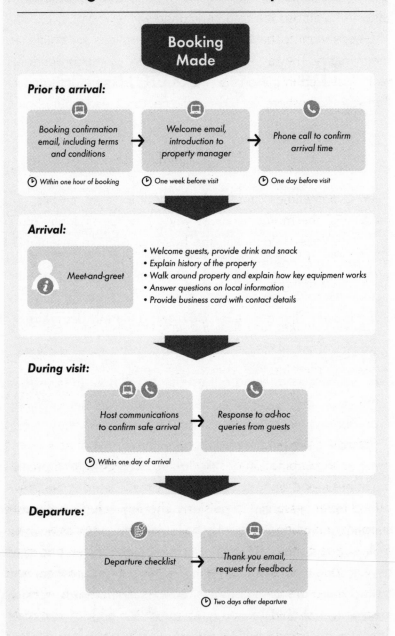

Booking Made

Prior to arrival:

Booking confirmation email, including terms and conditions
→
Welcome email, introduction to property manager
→
Phone call to confirm arrival time

Within one hour of booking   One week before visit   One day before visit

Arrival:

Meet-and-greet

- Welcome guests, provide drink and snack
- Explain history of the property
- Walk around property and explain how key equipment works
- Answer questions on local information
- Provide business card with contact details

During visit:

Host communications to confirm safe arrival
→
Response to ad-hoc queries from guests

Within one day of arrival

Departure:

Departure checklist
→
Thank you email, request for feedback

Two days after departure

leaving them in a positive frame of mind and willing to write you a great review. The diagram below shows the process we follow at Dantosa for communicating with guests.

Guests want to be sure that the expectations set online are met in reality. They expect to find the interior of your property just as it appeared in the online photos, so it is important to check that your homeshare contents replicate, or exceed, your photos.

WELCOME

After a sometimes lengthy back and forth of emails and messages, the moment comes when the guests finally arrive and meet face-to-face with the hosts, or their representative, and see the accommodation. Or, they manage to unlock the door after finding the hidden key.

> I always make sure that the fireplace is ready for my guests. That makes the place feel warm and inviting, relaxing after the long drive to get here.
>
> Ingrid, host from United States

Preparing the accommodation for the arrival of new guests involves a combination of stocktaking, shopping, and providing some mood-enhancing extras. As mentioned in the previous chapter, essential provisions should include bathroom supplies; cleaning materials; basic kitchen supplies such as milk, sugar, coffee, salt, pepper, olive oil, tea towels and oven gloves; and sports equipment, such as tennis rackets and balls if there are on-site sports facilities. If there is a working fireplace, it should be ready to go at the flick of a match. Some hosts include additional goodies to provide a warmer welcome – guests at Dantosa, for instance, find a hamper full of local produce. If the guests are arriving at night, the lights in the house should be switched on for ease of access, as well as providing a warm and welcoming glow.

> *Make house rules as clear as possible, at the time of the guest's arrival. This will ensure that guests know what is expected. In our description we say: we are not a hotel, we are inviting you into our home.*
>
> Howard, host from Hong Kong

Hosts have only one chance to make a good impression and that is more of a challenge if you are greeting your guests remotely.

> *When we meet a host for the first time, if they are warm and welcoming, we don't care about the front of their building, or that a wide-angle lens made their place look twice the size – or even if they forgot to mention they have four cats. We are just happy to be safe, and finally home.*
>
> Senior Nomads

THE PROPERTY MANAGER

Dantosa guests are met by a local manager, who lives a five-minute drive away. He contacts the guests 24 hours before their arrival to give them directions and the code to open the entrance gate, as well as answering any queries they may have, and arranges a meeting time. Sometimes, due to last-minute travel plan changes or delays, guests arrive and he is not yet there. For those occasions, interim welcome arrangements are in place. The manager will have texted them to let them know he is on the way, and in the meantime they will find the keys in the key safe, fresh flowers in the house and a welcome gift to get their stay off to a good start.

Other ways to welcome guests

The five senses approach: Some hosts provide a welcome that touches some or all of the five senses – for example:
- **hearing**: play music
- **smell**: bake bread or use a fragrant air freshener
- **touch**: offer a warm towel
- **taste**: provide a cheese platter and glass of wine
- **sight**: a seasonal flower arrangement

The personal pick-up: Some hosts pick up guests from the airport and provide them with a tour of the surrounding area and landmarks on their way to the property.

The virtual welcome: For hosts who are absent and without property managers, the meet-and-greet may take place via a welcoming email or text message.

When guests arrive at Dantosa, the property manager welcomes them warmly and gives them a tour of the property, including an explanation of how things work, such as the touch panels for lighting, the iPad-driven flat screen television and the central heating thermostats.

Prior to their arrival and following payment of the deposit, guests receive a confirmation email with more information about the property, and an email introduction to the property manager, telling them that he will be in touch soon to arrange access. Guests also receive a personalized welcome email from us on arrival. When they meet at the property, the property manager gives the guests a business card with his contact information in case they require assistance during their stay.

> *Every guest is different. Some want interaction with the host, others have come for their privacy. You need to be able to read them, to put yourself into their shoes, and respond accordingly.*
>
> Ingrid, host from United States

TIPS AND IDEAS
When contact can be critical
Providing multiple means of contact is recommended. As Airbnb guests ourselves in a Paris apartment during the 2015 terrorist attacks on the city, we found ourselves virtually abandoned. The owner did not contact us to check that we were safe, which was not very thoughtful. We realized that if we had been in a hotel, there would have been emergency response policies in place, but in the homeshare industry, these practices are not yet ingrained. For hosts, the bottom line is to treat guests in the same way you would treat anyone staying in your own home, and be warm, welcoming, and caring in the event of emergency situations.

> *I fund my overseas travel by homesharing. So for me, what is most difficult about hosting is always being online while out of the country to manage requests from guests.*
>
> Helen, host from Australia

GETTING TO KNOW YOU . . .

Some hosts pack up the entire contents of their home when they get a booking and take themselves off for a holiday. Others, especially those who are renting out a room or a floor in their house, like to stick around and get to know their guests. They may invite their guests out for a meal. Others drop in daily to say hello or to treat their guests to a special home-cooked meal. For some hosts, having guests stay is a way to supplement their social life, widen their horizons or chase away loneliness. For them, becoming a host can be a life-changing experience rather than just a way to earn some extra money. Empty-nest hosts may like to offer advice or get involved in their guests' activities, or even their lives. In some homes, the shared kitchen becomes a lively meeting point for guests of many nationalities and the hub of a genuine community. In a recent survey, hosts ranked meeting new people as the second best thing about hosting, after the income. As a host, it is up to you to set the limits and the ground rules for your guests. As the founders of Airbnb said at the annual Airbnb Open conference in November 2015, 'Even in middle America, you can now have the United Nations at your kitchen table.'

Nowadays, guests are familiar with the sharing economy concept, and on the whole are discreet and respectful of our home. They enjoy receiving personalized tips from us on what to explore and where to eat according to their taste and budget.

Romy, host from Hong Kong

WHAT COULD POSSIBLY GO WRONG?

ARRANGING KEY PICK-UPS

Key safes located on the property, when the guests have the access code, can be a secure way to provide keys, but it is not always possible to provide these. For example, in shared apartment buildings, hosts usually have no right to instal a key safe. An alternative is to find a trustworthy key holder, such as a friend or relative, who can be relied on to meet your guests on arrival. Another possibility is to arrange to leave a set of keys with a friendly café near the property or to use a service such as Igloohome (igloohome.co), which is endorsed by Airbnb and offers various key and security entry solutions designed for homeshares.

You can also consider putting the keys in a surfboard lock somewhere near the property. These are large, heavy padlocks opened by a combination code.

In some locations, key safe services are available, where homeshare hosts can centrally place their keys. The alternative keyless systems of locks with codes to open doors, which can be activated remotely, are another possible solution.

> **When things go wrong**
> One guest who spoke little English booked our Sydney apartment for a stay of several weeks. The guest only replied to our various emails and text messages 12 hours before arrival to make the arrangements to pick up the keys, which proved difficult to organize at such short notice. The keys were being held by an estate agent who needed to be instructed to release them, but we were unable to contact the agent in time to let him know that guests were arriving. After a long journey, and with a small

cranky baby in tow, the guests arrived at the agent's door in a taxi, tired and demanding the keys. The agent tried to contact us, but we were in Singapore – and in the middle of an electricity blackout that had just hit. Compounded by language communication difficulties, tempers flared, the guests caused a scene and the agent was upset. When we were finally reached, we managed to appease the guests by refunding some of their money and paying their taxi fare, but the incident resulted in the agent refusing to manage the apartment keys for future guests.

Anticipate issues and assume that guests do not read your instructions before arrival. I have now put up a sign 'please do not park in front of the garage' as many guests would park their cars so that I could not drive out of my garage. Instead of welcoming them, I would start by asking them to move their car, which was not a good beginning to their visit.

Ingrid, host from the United States

AMBIGUOUS INSTRUCTIONS

Professional hosts are typically clear and specific with guests about the conditions for using their property and its facilities, but that is not always the case. In one Hong Kong property, guests were told that the 'key was under the mat' and that they should present themselves to the building manager as 'friends of the owners'. The hosts were unclear about whether the guests could use the swimming pool and gym facilities in the building and seemed unsure about what the access codes were. Be precise about information such as key codes, key locations, and what is and is not included in the rental price so that guests know exactly what to expect.

It is also important to be clear about what services, if any, can be arranged at additional cost. For example, long-stay guests may request regular cleaning services during their stay. If hosts can arrange this, they should ensure the costs are known and agreed to by the guests in advance to avoid misunderstandings after their arrival.

TRACKING ARRIVALS

In one case, guests arriving at the Sydney apartment were on a flight that was delayed for eight hours. As the guests could not communicate by phone or internet while they were on the plane, we were left in the dark about what was happening and had no idea of the guests' new arrival time until shortly after touchdown, when we finally received a text from them. Taking a tip from hotels who typically ask guests for their flight arrival details, we now always ask for the flight number so that we can track the plane's arrival time.

> *Several times a host has met us with their car, or helped us with our luggage from the train or bus station to their home. Having the host, or a trusted surrogate, meet us for this last leg of our journey is one of the nicest welcomes we could ask for.*
>
> Senior Nomads

Expect the unexpected

As a host, it is wise to expect unusual requests, and not to be surprised if something out of the ordinary occurs. Be empathetic and try to put yourself in your guests' shoes;

anticipate their questions and needs. Sometimes, though, even the best preparations can't deal with every complication. That's when there is no replacement for human resourcefulness. One booking at Dantosa saw the arrival of a group of 16 guests who were planning to do a lot of home cooking. But on the first evening, the oven stopped working just as they were about to put their carefully prepared lasagne inside. It proved impossible to get the oven repaired or to hire a replacement oven in time to cook their meal. The property manager therefore drove over, took the lasagne and cooked it in his own oven, then brought it back to the house for the guests to eat.

We once received a last-minute booking for Dantosa following a tragedy in the guest's family. It was agreed that payment in full would be made to the property manager as soon as the guests arrived at the house. The sum owed was about US$6,000. We were expecting payment to be made by credit card, but the guests arrived with the full amount of cash in hand, which they presented to the property manager. Taken aback, he accepted the money, sent us a photograph of the cash and banked it.

Strive for service excellence. This is especially so when there are issues. Be contactable, friendly, accommodating and very helpful in providing a fast and acceptable solution or workaround.

Ricci, host from Hong Kong and Malaysia

MANAGING EXPECTATIONS: A HOTEL OR A HOMESHARE?

For you, it's your home, your holiday home, or a room in your home. For a guest, it's nothing less than a hotel and their expectations of what's on offer may be high. In fact, the better your website and the higher your online ranking, the more guests will expect in terms of service, facilities and professionalism. Some guests expect a homeshare to provide minibars, pick-up service and laundry services. To avoid setting expectations higher than you can actually manage, ensure that your description of the services you offer is accurate and honest about what you can and can't provide.

> *The key challenges of hosting are dealing with guests who do not respect your property and who leave the place messy. People sometimes think we are a hotel and expect the moon, which can be tricky to manage.*
>
> Sidharth, host from India

Guests often forget that a homeshare is, by its very nature, very different from a hotel stay. For instance, a hotel may have 20 or more identical rooms on offer, and if one is not available or cleaning is delayed, they can usually offer guests an alternative. Homeshares have no such flexibility, and are rarely able to offer alternative accommodation if a problem arises.

Table manners

One guest at our Sydney apartment was adamant they needed a tablecloth for the dining table, which was one of the few things we had not thought to provide. At the time, Derek was several thousand miles away, so he arranged for his father to cross Sydney to deliver a table-cloth to them.

Even our 16-year-old daughter now enjoys hosting, despite having to occasionally share her bathroom with total strangers.

Romy, host from Hong Kong

COMMUNICATIONS DURING THE VISIT

During your guests' stay, it is important that they feel 'in safe hands'. While a formal concierge service is not viable for most home stays, it is sensible to anticipate your guests' needs and questions. Many homeshare hosts provide written information for their guests in the form of an information pack or welcome kit. It is also recommended that you provide guests with a contact phone number which can be used at any time. Most guests will not abuse this, and it does open the lines of communication for you with your guests.

You need to get the communications balance right. For each guest, gauge the level of assistance that they will require or would like. Some guests are self-sufficient and would see more than an email or a call as intrusive during their visit. Others are keen to obtain advice about your neighbourhood and may want regular contact during their stay.

One family who stayed with us was from the UK and they had children of the same age as ours. We all hit it off and made friends; we spent the whole weekend with them, going to the aquarium and the park. Our children stay in touch with theirs and will have a place to stay in the UK if they ever go there . . .

Megan, host from United States

INFORMATION PACKS

Time is required to provide local information, tourist guides and transport information, as unlike at a hotel, there is no concierge, so you need to anticipate your guests' questions.

Helen, host from Australia

Inside the Dantosa property, guests will find an information pack designed to help them make the most of the property and the local area. The Dantosa welcome guide includes instructions on how to operate appliances and troubleshooting; details of the onsite facilities; suggested activities nearby or onsite, and recommendations in the surrounding area for restaurants, cafés, shopping, galleries, bushwalking and tourist sites. The pack also includes practical information, such as what to do if the electricity fails. You can see what we include on page 75.

We are always grateful when there is a house manual. In Paris, if our host hadn't noted that the kitchen light switch was awkwardly located behind the refrigerator, and the best way to reach it was with the handle of the wooden spoon he kept on the counter just for that purpose, we would have been left in the dark.

Senior Nomads

Information Pack – Table of Contents
Dantosa Blue Mountains Retreat

Information packs can start small and be built up gradually. At Dantosa, the recommendations started as a list of our own favourite restaurants and activities, and expanded over time to include answers to commonly asked questions on amenities and local activities. For example, after one group on a corporate retreat requested an archery activity, the information pack now includes team-building activities for guests.

Providing a local guide with information about your neighbourhood is very important and helps guests enjoy their visit. You are sharing your local insights and ensuring they experience the best that your town has to offer.

Yvonne, host from France and Australia

DEPARTURE

While it may not be as important as their arrival, your guests' departure also needs to be managed carefully, leaving them with a positive impression. At Dantosa, a departure checklist (see below) is included in the welcome kit, to assist guests when they leave. Remind guests to check for any lost property and explain your lock-up procedures clearly. You also need to consider how to politely ensure that your guests leave on time, so that your next transition can be conducted on schedule.

Dantosa Blue Mountains Retreat
Departure Checklist

- ☑ Return the keys to the keysafe box
- ☑ Turn off the heating
- ☑ Turn off the lights
- ☑ Turn on the dishwasher if there is dirty crockery
- ☑ Empty the refrigerator and freezer
- ☑ Check for any forgotten belongings
- ☑ Take any excess garbage with you
- ☑ Join us on Facebook and Instagram
- ☑ Provide us with feedback

Summary

- Become a homeshare guest yourself to 'live the experience' and to learn what to do and what not to do.

- Ensure you have spare keys, as guests often forget to return them when they leave.

- First impressions count; make sure that your homeshare is ready when your guests arrive.

- Ensure that guests have a reliable way to contact you or your local representative during their visit.

- If you are an absent host, include a departure checklist for your guests.

- Expect the unexpected and be a creative problem-solver.

- Remember the hotel rule: the guest is always right.

5

The Art of Transitions

A successful homeshare business relies on efficient transitions between guests. In homeshare terms, a transition is the period between the departure of one guest and the arrival of the next one. As all hotel managers know, perfecting a streamlined process to clean and prepare rooms for the next guest results in higher occupancy rates and increased profit. The same is true for homeshares, but the process is more complex because unlike hotels, most hosts do not have cleaning and maintenance teams at their disposal. Allow time to fine-tune the transition process when you are starting your homeshare business. Many new hosts allow a full day between guests to make sure everything goes smoothly.

Remember, hosts only get one chance to make a great first impression, so ensure the homeshare is completely ready for each new guest.

THE IMPORTANCE OF CLEANING

Cleaning is an essential part of a successful transition and it should be carried out to the highest possible standard. In a recent survey (see overleaf), hosts rated cleaning as the greatest homesharing challenge, three times higher than the next options, of sales or calendar management.

What is your greatest challenge as a host?

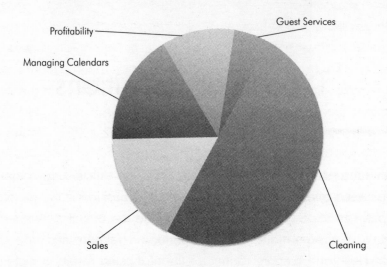

Cleaning homeshares is different to cleaning your own home. Typically, a homeshare has less clutter than the average home, and a higher level of attention to detail is required to prepare a homeshare. Preparing it for new guests involves more than just cleaning and changing linen. It should also include a walk-through at the end of the cleaning and preparation process, to check each room and inspect it from the perspective of a guest. If you are hiring cleaners, it is important that they understand this distinctive process.

> *Make your home squeaky clean!*
> Ricci, host from Hong Kong and Malaysia

Your guests should feel that the rooms and supplies are completely clean and fresh and have been prepared especially for their stay. The homeshare should feel cleaner than their own home. If you are doing the cleaning yourself, do research to find the best products and cleaning methods for your needs and learn how to clean brilliantly. If the thought of cleaning to a consistently high standard overwhelms you, get help or consider outsourcing the job to an expert, or a team of professional cleaners.

Get into the habit of cleaning or arranging a clean as soon as a guest leaves, even if the next guest is not scheduled to arrive for some time. This will allow you to accept any last-minute bookings with confidence that the place is ready. If there is a gap of more than a few days before your next guest arrives, schedule a final walk-through just before their arrival to ensure that the homeshare is still looking fresh and clean. Guests can tell if a room has been locked up and disused for a while before their visit. Dust surfaces, remove any dead insects on the floor and use an air freshener to remove any musty smells.

SEAMLESS TRANSITIONS

Achieving seamless transitions will mainly depend on preparing – and following – a complete checklist for each part of the property and then ensuring an adequate timeline for cleaning and maintenance between stays. Take a tip from hotels. They have perfected the art of efficient transitions and do so with the help of well-documented processes and staff training. Consider training your cleaners to ensure that they can perform the work required to your standards. Make sure that your cleaners use the checklists you have prepared and stress that they must not cut corners in their work.

Cleaning the chateau between guests is a huge task and takes 16 hours of work, excluding the laundry. You have to be very organized and have good staff to rely on.

Yvonne, host from France and Australia

This can happen inadvertently. Once at our Sydney apart-ment, not all the bed linen was changed between guests. The cleaner mistakenly thought one of the beds had not been used and so did not change the sheets. This oversight only came to light when the next guest complained.

Start by preparing a checklist of what needs to be done in each room of your homeshare (you can find a sample on p. 83), together with photographs of the completed work. Specify every step required to get the room ready. This includes cleaning, arranging furniture, making beds, checking equip-ment and lights, providing supplies, refilling soap containers, taking out rubbish, documenting any damage and missing items, and making an inventory of the fixtures and fittings. This will help you to streamline the transition process regardless of who is doing it, and will be a great help in calculating how long each room will take to prepare and for briefing a new cleaning team. If needed, remember to include arranging a flower display, preparing a fruit bowl, writing a welcome card, and placing chocolates on pillows. Include a list for the garden and external areas of your homeshare if you have them. Guests will be disappointed if your home is beautifully presented, but your outdoor lights are not working or the lawns are overgrown.

To ensure that transitions work well, I created a detailed instruction list that includes the position of the furniture, instructions for hanging the towels in the bathroom and folding additional towels creatively on the beds, how to display the chocolates and wine that are set out on the dining room table, and the special fold required for the toilet paper.

Brianna, host from Australia

Transition Checklist for Dantosa House
ROOM: Bedroom 2

Bed

- ☐ Queen: White bedding with dark runner and 3 cushions
- ☐ Queen bed is in position, slightly off centre to allow access to hanging cupboard
- ☐ Ensure that mattress is aligned on base

Windows

- ☐ White door blind works well
- ☐ White door blind is left up (10cm drop)
- ☐ Window shutter blinds are down and open

Lights

- ☐ Check bedside lamps are working (plugged in and bulbs operational)
- ☐ Check ceiling light works
- ☐ 4 unused power points switched off

Doors

- ☐ Door handle works and door handle closes properly
- ☐ Door is left wide open
- ☐ Glass sliding doors are locked

Furniture

- ☐ Bedside table drawers are empty and clean
- ☐ Cushion in window seat is clean and has zipper hidden (against wall)
- ☐ Cupboard with shelves is empty and clean
- ☐ Cupboard with hanging space is empty and clean
- ☐ Heater is put away inside hanging cupboard with cord rolled tidily
- ☐ 12 wooden, matching coat hangers are hanging tidily

Cleaning

- ☐ Vacuum entire room, including inside cupboards
- ☐ Wipe down all surfaces with damp microfibre cloth
- ☐ Empty wastepaper basket

Asset register

- ☐ Queen bed with 4 pillows
- ☐ 3 cushions
- ☐ 1 heater
- ☐ 1 fitted cushion for window seat
- ☐ 12 wooden matching coat hangers
- ☐ 2 bedside tables
- ☐ 2 bedside lamps
- ☐ 2 pictures above the bed

LOST AND FOUND

Identify any items left behind by previous guests so you can return them. This care with belongings will not go unnoticed and is likely to lead to a good review and perhaps a return visit.

TIPS AND IDEAS
Costing the cleaning
Remember to include the cost of cleaning in your pricing. If you are using hired cleaners to do the job, ensure that you have calculated the correct cost for their services, including extra or higher charges for working on week-ends or evenings to avoid any unwelcome surprises later.

If you are doing the cleaning yourself, you can use the rate charged by professional cleaning companies to help calculate the cost. Regardless of whether you are doing the cleaning or hiring someone to do it for you, remember to charge the cost of cleaning to your guests.

TIMING TRANSITIONS

The length of time needed to carry out a transition will vary depending on the size of your homeshare and the scale of homeshare operation you are running. To work out how long a standard transition will take, carry out every item on your checklist and time how long it takes you to complete the work. Include non-cleaning jobs, such as shopping for fresh supplies and changing bed linen and towels. You will then have a good idea of the amount of time required to complete a transition single-handed. For every additional person preparing the property, the transition time required will be shorter – if a transition takes four hours, then two people working together should be able to finish the job in two hours.

When scheduling transitions, allow an extra hour or two as a buffer between guests to cover particularly difficult cleaning or to fix any unexpected damage. When you are starting out, be realistic and allow plenty of time to transition your homeshare. You can reduce your 'transition window' as your confidence in the cleaning process increases.

The critical element in managing tight transitions is to ensure that departing guests leave on time. Set a definite check-out time and make sure your guests are aware of it. Few things are more stressful than trying to clean around departing guests while knowing the arrival of new guests is imminent.

HIRING A TRANSITION TEAM

Outsourcing the management of our homeshare business has been a great option for us. Our manager is responsible for sales, the guest experience and transitions between visits.

Sue, host from United Kingdom

If you plan to employ a cleaner, a team of cleaners or a cleaning company, careful planning and co-ordination will be required. First of all, allow time to find and hire the right people. Outsourcing will mean finding cleaners that are reliable, available at the times you need them and who have excellent cleaning skills. Ask for recommendations, and be prepared to step in yourself to do the work in the meantime.

Once you have found the right cleaning team, establish with them a clear timetable for transitions so that your cleaner is aware of the exact time of each departure and subsequent arrival. If you are not going to be on the premises yourself, set up a system under which they report back to you once a clean is complete. If you outsource your cleaning to a company, try to make sure that the same cleaners come to your homeshare each time. This will ensure they become familiar with your rooms and with the specific tasks required, and will also be able to quickly assess whether something is missing or broken.

> In the early days, I had different cleaners and managed some of the transitions myself. The nature of the cleaning business tends to be transient so it's tough to find a reliable cleaner. Now that my homeshare business has escalated, I employ a cleaner for each transition; I have particularly high standards and trained her myself. I maintain the garden, deal with administration and business development. It's a better use of my time.
>
> James, host from Australia

The transition team needs to report back to you on the state of the homeshare soon after each guest's visit, and inform you of any items that are missing or broken. This reckoning must be done as soon as possible after each guest departs. If you only realize weeks after a visit that an item is missing or broken, it will be difficult to identify which guest was responsible and to claim damages from them.

I had some young guests damage my dishwasher which I didn't discover until weeks later as I was not there on check-out. I had to replace the whole unit and claim on my household insurance.

Helen, host from Australia

AVOIDING THE PERILS OF OUTSOURCING

Outsourcing transitions can be difficult, particularly if you are a remote host. It can take some time to find the right team. Detailed and frank communication is vital from the outset to avoid misunderstandings about how and for what you will be charged. If your transition partner prefers to charge by the hour, they may take longer to complete the cleaning, which will increase your costs and affect the efficiency of turnarounds. Ensure that you agree in advance the cost of a standard clean and also agree on charges for additional cleaning.

Finding a person who can clean efficiently and is present-able to conduct meet-and-greet with guests is tough. They are two very different skill sets.

Yvonne, host from France and Australia

Consider offering your cleaners a bonus payment if you exceed your occupancy goals, or if you receive frequent comments from guests on how clean and well presented your homeshare is.

I worked with the cleaning teams for two or three transitions to ensure each property was delivered on time, on budget and to the required quality. While the effort required to select and train the right team was significant,

*it was worthwhile, as I can now focus on driving occu-
pancy, with the peace of mind that the transitions will
occur effortlessly.*

Brianna, host from Australia

It is important that your cleaners feel connected to your
homeshare and are encouraged to be proud of their work. Tell
them how crucial their role is to the guest experience. Hosts
can help to build this inclusion and sense of ownership in their
cleaning team by making them feel part of the business, for
example by sharing guest reviews with them and involving
them in problem-solving.

*A mentally disabled woman does my cleaning. This
arrangement is good for me as I don't have to do heavy
lifting and it provides her with an income.*

Ingrid, host from United States

MAINTAINING QUALITY WHEN OUTSOURCING TRANSITIONS

Making sure that each transition is performed to the same
high standard is not easy, especially when the job is outsourced
to a third party. Take the following steps to minimize potential
problems:

- Communicate your expectations clearly to your transition team
  from the first meeting, and provide checklists and photographs.
- Conduct a transition together with your cleaners so you can
  show them how you like work done and can comment on
  the finished work.
- Ask for reports after each transition, including before-
  and-after photos and a list of any damaged or missing
  items.

- Manage supplies yourself, at least at the outset.
- If using a cleaning company, request that the same cleaners attend your homeshare each time, so they become familiar with the property.
- Conduct spot checks; visit the property unannounced to check quality after a transition has been completed.
- Consider using an app like Properly (www.getproperly.com) to communicate with your cleaner.

I do a surprise pop-in on my cleaners, to see how transitions are going and to thank them.

Brianna, host from Australia

TIPS AND IDEAS
Managing distant transitions
For distant hosts like us, managing the 120 transitions each year at our Blue Mountains property has been challenging. We have agreed a contract with our current transition team that stipulates the scope, the time required and the cost of a standard transition, as well as rates for additional cleaning. We hold a monthly operational call to discuss guest reviews, upcoming bookings and any maintenance requirements. Ad-hoc communication with the transition manager is usually conducted via WhatsApp or email.

Back-to-back bookings on the same day can be difficult to manage. We are lucky to have reliable, well-trained local staff who are available at short notice.

Sidharth, host from India

MAINTENANCE

Scheduling regular property maintenance is an important part of keeping your property in top condition. Even if your guests take good care of your property, the general wear and tear in a homeshare is much greater than it would be in a home. Conduct regular spring cleaning, repairs and maintenance at times between guest visits and block out these dates in your calendars. Ensure that you have booked any required repair workers ahead of time to make full use of the blocked-out period. Arrange for maintenance to take place during your quiet periods to minimize any loss of business.

MANAGING SUPPLIES

Keeping stock of your homeshare supplies is important. Do you have enough toilet paper for the next guest? Are your soap containers filled? Did the last guests use up all the cooking supplies? Do you have the cleaning supplies you need for the next five transitions? Is your vacuum cleaner working properly? Inventory management principles apply in the same way as if you were running a shop. You do not want to have to run to the supermarket minutes before a guest arrives to buy more soap powder, so you need to develop a checklist to keep track of what supplies you have and when you need to buy more. If you are an absent host, then you may need to rely on your cleaners to manage supplies for you. Ensure that this process is running smoothly and conduct spot checks to see how supplies are stocked.

Some supplies cannot be purchased far ahead of guest visits. If you plan to provide fresh milk, flowers, a fruit bowl or a cheese platter, these will need to be bought just before the guests arrive, so remember to leave time in your transitions planning for that.

TIPS AND IDEAS
Bulk buying and storage
Buying non-perishable items in bulk where possible will reduce overall costs. Remember to make sure that you have enough storage in a place that guests can't access.

At Dantosa, a walk-in pantry has been transformed into a supplies cupboard. It holds light bulbs, torch batteries, firelighters, toilet paper, additional matching crockery and glassware, pre-assembled welcome hampers containing local produce, linen and towels, as well as bathroom, kitchen and laundry supplies. Guests have no access to this area; it can only be accessed by the hosts and their transition team, and supplies are checked regularly.

LINEN

Bed linen is best bought in sets of three for each bed. This enables you to have one set of clean linen ready for the incoming guest, one set of dirty linen to wash from the past guest, and one spare set.

Most homeshares provide guests with towels. At Dantosa, bath towels are provided for each guest, and hand towels and bathmats are provided in each bathroom. Ensure that there are some spare towels available for guests should they need them. Again, three sets of towels are advisable so that washing between guest visits is not onerous.

Ensure that your transition process includes the management of linen. Allow time to wash and iron linen between visits. Decide whether to wash linen on site in your own laundry, or to outsource the job. If you use a third party to provide clean linen, check the quality of their linen and make sure they provide a reliable collection and drop-off service.

Always store spare linen as back-up at your homeshare, preferably in a locked cupboard. You don't want to be caught short during transitions.

TIPS AND IDEAS
Remember the towels
Purchase high-quality linen and towels; they will not only last longer, but will also be noticed and enjoyed by your guests. Hotel research indicates that the two items most appreciated by guests are a comfortable bed and high-quality towels.

PREPARING A PLAN B

For your peace of mind, try to work out a back-up transition solution. If your cleaner is ill or unavailable at the last minute, what will you do? If you are unable to manage the transition yourself, who can you call at short notice?

Even the best-laid plans can run into unforeseen problems. Once at Dantosa, the manager called to say that because of snow, some of his team were unable to carry out the transition cleaning. Derek happened to be in the neighbourhood and was able to go to the property and work with the available team members to carry out a successful transition. The experience made him realize that it is important to have back-up transition resources.

OUT-OF-THE-BOX SOLUTIONS

Be creative with solutions if you know that a transition may be problematic. A host in Greece who knew that his homeshare would not be ready on time picked Gabriela up from the airport, took her for a drive around the island, then suggested she breakfast at a local café while he took care of her luggage. He returned to collect her a few hours later once the homeshare was ready. He realized that this experience was preferable to her arriving at the homeshare while it was being cleaned.

Too tight a transition window may mean guests arrive before the property is ready. If that happens, look for innovative solutions. On one occasion, Derek had offered a later check-out to departing guests, and realized too late that the next guest's arrival time gave the transition team only 90 minutes to turn around the large property. He offered the guest a bag drop-off service and dinner at a local restaurant. The guest was thrilled to have a free dinner at a well-regarded local restaurant, and the transition team had time to finish their work.

Summary

- Create a transition checklist for each room of your homeshare.

- Allow extra buffer time between visits when you first start.

- Communicate clearly and in detail with your transition team to ensure efficient transitions and help maximize occupancy rates.

- Prepare a back-up plan for cleaning your property between guests.

- Ensure you know the cost of a transition, including overtime and other charges.

- Ensure guests know their check-out time, and establish a procedure to make sure that they leave on time.

6

Guest Reviews – The Good, the Bad and the Ugly

Guest reviews are an invaluable resource. They are a way of seeing your homeshare from the other side of the mirror. They let you look from the outside in, and see how your property is viewed from the perspective of your guests. This makes them a unique resource for learning about your business and improving your service in the ways that are most meaningful to guests. Positive reviews and high ratings from your guests build confidence in prospective guests and lead to more bookings. Reviews that are not so positive help you to learn what your guests need and how to improve your business.

> *Any review is a good review. Even if the rating is low, you can learn from this feedback and improve.*
>
> Mitch, host from Australia

Reviews provide direct and often detailed feedback on what is working and what is not working for your guests. That super-soft bed you thought your guests would enjoy could turn out to be causing them backache. Your thoughtfully equipped kitchen could prove to be inadequate for guests who prefer Asian dishes. If something is missing, reviews are a good way of letting you know. Reviews can also show you how even the smallest or lowest-cost items – high-quality towels, luggage racks, well-sharpened kitchen knives – can turn out to make a real difference to your guests' experience.

It takes time to develop a good attitude to reviews. We initially underestimated their importance, both to potential guests and as a means of learning more about the homeshare business. Now, we see them as an essential and valuable resource for building and improving the appeal of our properties.

> We were delighted when one guest wrote: 'Amazing! Perfect location, superb standard of house. Everything was spot on!'
>
> Tom, host from Croatia and Sweden

HOW REVIEWS WORK

Reviews comprise two elements – a rating, typically a score from 1 to 5, and free-format comments. The ratings system is a simple way of sorting and comparing properties, especially for prospective guests. Comments are more laborious to analyze and may not be read or used by as many people as the ratings. Additionally, some online travel agencies offer guests the opportunity to provide private feedback to the host, such as suggestions for improvement, which are not viewed by the wider community.

Every online travel agency has its own review system. Airbnb's rating is based on six criteria: cleanliness, accuracy of listing, arrival, location, communications and value. On the Australian site Stayz, reviews are based on cleanliness, comfort, location and quality. Unlike any other online travel agency, both guests and hosts can provide reviews on Airbnb and this seems to encourage a higher number of reviews.

Reviews are read by all members of the homeshare community – prospective guests looking for a property to stay in, guests who want to see what hosts have written about them, hosts who read reviews of themselves and of their competitors, online travel agencies who monitor reviews for appropriateness and language and, in the case of Airbnb, to designate Superhosts. Businesses also read reviews to select accommodation for their employees, and prospective buyers of homeshare properties use reviews to shortlist potential purchases.

Online reviews are a step up from the traditional guest book that was once found in most small hotels and bed and breakfast accommodation. We keep a guest book at Dantosa, but as absent hosts, we rarely see the comments people write. And because it is a guest book, guests seem constrained in their comments and tend to write remarks that are kind but vague (for example, 'What a beautiful property'), without enlightening the host about what could be improved. Online reviews by contrast are usually more structured and precise about what was good and what could be better. Unlike a guest book, they are accessible to prospective guests, who value reviews as an informed and independent assessment of the property.

Reviews are also a useful marketing tool. Snippets of comments from happy guests make great additions to your marketing materials and legitimize your property descriptions. Actively seeking reviews and responding to guest suggestions is a great way to improve your guests' experience and build your homeshare brand.

Suggestions from guests are always welcome. I like to speak with a guest after their visit, to obtain feedback. We have made changes as a result of guest comments, such as installing a full-length mirror in our apartment.

Brianna, host from Australia

MORE REVIEWS = MORE BUSINESS

Encouraging your guests to leave reviews is extremely important. As well as giving you more feedback, search engine optimization often works by volume, so the more reviews you have, the higher up the list your property will be displayed. Many hosts openly ask their guests to give them a good review if they have been happy with their visit. About 90% of guests who stay at Dantosa now provide reviews, up from under 20% in the first year.

Additionally, in the event that you receive an atypically unfair review, the overall number of reviews will show that this review is an outlier. Obtaining as many reviews as possible will help to water down the impact of an unusually poor review.

Hosts can remind guests by email or with a phone call to post a review. We have found that requesting reviews by phoning the guest is often successful. A personal phone call often results in a review that is more specific and honest than a response provided to an automated email request for feedback. And remember the importance of a smooth and thoughtful departure – this is the last memory your guests will take away with them about their time at your property, and it often makes its way into their review. Hosts can also request a review in person during the check-out process, which can be very effective.

Homesharing has been a great experience for our children. It's a family business and our children help. We have a transition checklist and they sometimes do jobs (e.g. put coffee in the machine, dust surfaces) and they feel pride for the work they have put in. We read the guest reviews together so they learn to receive feedback.

Megan, host from United States

Most guests post reviews soon after their stay. The immediacy of the feedback means you can quickly respond to suggestions and improvements, and post your own updates and responses to show that you are listening to your guests and taking action in response to their experience. That is the kind of service that can make the difference between being a good host and a Superhost.

What is a Superhost?

Airbnb offers a Superhost status based partly on the excellence of guest reviews. The Airbnb Superhost category can be used as a search filter by prospective guests seeking the best levels of service. Hosts who gain the status can use a special Superhost symbol on their homeshare listing. Superhosts benefit from an enhanced support service, are invited to beta-test new offerings, and may be eligible for discounts for various services. The Superhost category is fast becoming a distinguishing factor on Airbnb and can lead to many more bookings. Superhost status is reviewed quarterly by Airbnb and is renewed only if hosts continue to perform well on rankings.

Most online travel agents have a formal review process and encourage guests to review their stay. Each online travel agency has its own approach to reviews and it is worth spending time to find out how they work. For example, Airbnb provides a very quick review process based on specific criteria and – unlike most online travel agencies – encourages two-way feedback – from host to guest, and from guest to host. Airbnb guest reviews are only posted online publicly after the host has reviewed the guest, or after two weeks. This is designed to encourage hosts to review their guests quickly.

This approach is part of Airbnb's focus on building a home-share community where continual improvements and innovations are encouraged based on constructive feedback on both sides. Other sites emphasize the interaction between host and guest as more of a transaction than participation in a community. That change in relationship can influence the review. The personal touch in the culture of Airbnb homeshares tends to encourage more forgiving and generous reviews.

Reviewing your guests

When we leave a review of our Airbnb guests, we take care to include the name of their property, to promote it to other hosts who may themselves be interested in staying sometime in the future. This two-way review process has both pros and cons:

- *Positives*: It creates a sense of community, encourages reviews and establishes a respectful culture. Airbnb also enforces community standards and can remove hosts and guests who repeatedly receive poor reviews.

- *Negatives*: It can encourage people to leave inflated ratings in the hope that their own rating will then be positive.

ENCOURAGING GOOD REVIEWS

To improve your chances of getting a good review, first focus on getting as many reviews as possible. According to Airbnb, only 2–10% of guests at large hotels leave written reviews, but 70–75% of Airbnb guests provide reviews for their hosts. Aim to achieve close to 100% of guests leaving a review.

Ensure that there is a way to capture reviews for guests who do not make a booking through an online travel agency that offers review opportunities. Consider adding a link to your property's website if you have one.

Go the extra mile in your service – personal touches are remembered and will be mentioned in the reviews. When you do get good reviews, always thank the guest publicly for their review. This is a good way to encourage others to do the same.

It is worth the effort to try to get the best reviews you can. Positive reviews are encouraging and justify the work and effort spent on getting them. Hosts experience a buzz of excitement every time their status as Airbnb Superhosts is announced. It is an external endorsement of the excellence of service that gives hosts a sense of a job well done, and pushes them to maintain and improve their standards and service.

It's very rewarding to provide a good service that a guest has really enjoyed. I often get comments like 'We don't want to leave'. Some of my guests come four times a year.

James, host from Australia

MANAGING POOR REVIEWS

Bad reviews can lead to a loss of business. Lower ratings will also affect the ranking order of your property listing. For example, on Stayz, higher ratings ensure your property is displayed on the site's first page.

We recall the long-lasting impact of a poor review when Dantosa Cottage was first listed separately and received a three-star rating because of a lack of cooking equipment and problems with the cable TV and WiFi. We lost our Superhost status for one quarter and it took some time before the cottage was booked again.

Attention to detail and managing expectations are essential to ensuring positive reviews. Make clear decisions about what you are going to provide, and then let your guests know. For example, if you have a tennis court, either provide tennis racquets and balls, or set expectations that you are not going to provide tennis equipment.

Always do your best as a host, go in with a good heart, but don't take reviews personally. Some people are complainers (the minority) and will find something wrong . . . one of our guests liked the place but requested an essential oil infuser. If you go out and buy every obscure item that anyone wants you'll spend a fortune.

Megan, host from United States

However, even with the greatest care, things can go wrong. A poor review sometimes results when everything has gone beautifully – with one exception. It only takes one thing to go wrong and that will be what the guest remembers. But every problem brings opportunities. The host's response to a critical review can be more than enough to reassure potential guests that the host is responsive and takes action to correct short-comings – the best sign of service excellence.

Occasionally, negative reviews are posted that are inaccurate, or that are the result of a misunderstanding. For example, we recall one case where a guest claimed that no tea towels had been provided when in fact they had. On such occasions, you still need to respond and be polite. It is best to post a public response, thanking the guest for the review but also clarifying the position, such as: *'Thank you for your feedback. Ordinarily we do provide six tea towels in the top kitchen drawer and we will ensure that these are always there in future. Apologies for the inconvenience.'*

Remember, all reviews are essentially useful feedback and are likely to be good for business. They add visibility to your property, and provide opportunities to promote or improve your business. We have made many changes to our own properties based on suggestions made in reviews and have learned a lot about the homeshare business on the way. So don't take comments personally. Stay fact-based, and don't react emotionally to poor reviews.

But remember too that you can't win them all. In some cases, even when hosts have been honest and upfront about what to expect, guests' expectations exceed what is possible.

Responding to reviews – public or private?

Some online travel agencies provide the option to respond both privately and publicly to the guest, and the host should definitely take the opportunity to respond. When we received a poor rating for Dantosa Cottage, we sent the guest a private email apologizing for the deficiencies outlined and committing to taking action to resolve the problems. We also offered a reduced rate if the guest ever wanted to return. On the public forum, we thanked the guest for their recommendations and listed the actions we would take to rectify the situation, including dates by which they would be completed. When responding to subsequent guests, we mentioned that we hoped the guest had enjoyed the new facilities provided. We also updated the description of the cottage to reflect the changes.

Summary

- Guest reviews are important for your business – ignore them at your peril.

- Guest reviews offer a great opportunity to promote your homeshare and to find out how to enhance your guest experience and business results.

- If you receive criticism, don't be defensive. Remember, most guests who take the time to provide a review are hoping you will read their comments with an open mind and are not vindictive.

- Learn how the review process works for the online travel agencies you are using, so you can guide guests in how to leave an online review.

- With Airbnb, hosts can also leave a review of their guests. This is important to do if you want to contribute to the homeshare community.

Part Three
The Business of Homeshare

7

Financial Management

Preparing your home, reaching your audience and managing your online presence are essential steps to running a successful homeshare business, but if you fail to keep a close eye on the numbers once the bookings start coming in, you can easily lose track of your expenses and end up with an unprofitable business. Financial management is crucial to your homeshare business, whether you're offering a space on your couch or a large luxury estate.

> From visiting other people's homeshare properties, I see many people doing it half-heartedly. Run it strictly as a business, not as a hobby, and aim high.
>
> James, host from Australia

Keeping good records is essential in case someone else needs to step in and take over the business temporarily or in an emergency, for example in case of illness. If you are planning to sell your homeshare business at a later date, complete financial records will make the process much easier.

Regardless of the size of your business, you should keep your basic accounts up to date. As well as managing your tax liability and finding out whether your business is making money, good financial management creates a valuable resource to help you to cut costs and identify possible growth areas for your homeshare.

> *One of the greatest challenges for us is the changing tax laws.*
>
> Sue, host from the UK

DO IT YOURSELF OR GET EXPERT HELP?

The principles of managing income and expenditure remain the same whatever the size of your homeshare business. Some aspects, such as monitoring expenses, you will easily be able to manage yourself once you have disciplined yourself to keep accounts carefully. For other parts of your financial management cycle, such as preparing tax returns, you may choose to seek advice from an accountant. The level of tax you need to pay will vary according to the size of your business and the rules in your tax jurisdiction, which can vary widely from country to country. While no one enjoys the prospect of paying tax, the key principle to bear in mind is to ensure that you are able to pay it; a tax bill means your business is making a profit, so look on your tax liability as a good sign.

For large-scale homeshare businesses involving two or more properties that are devoted to homeshares, you may want to consider setting up a company structure. This can enable you to handle your financial management more efficiently and cost-effectively. You will need to take advice from an accountant in your jurisdiction who can advise you on the pros and cons of this decision.

If your business is small, you may use a spreadsheet or opt for an online book-keeping system to organize your accounts.

Many programs are available, ranging from basic to sophisticated. Ask your accountant for a recommendation.

GETTING ORGANIZED

In a recent survey (see below), 86% of hosts stated that the primary reason that they managed a homeshare was to earn money. If you plan to build a viable business that makes money, you will need to adopt a professional mindset about your homeshare. Focus on the needs of the business and work as if someone else will one day be taking it over.

What is the main reason that you are a homeshare host?

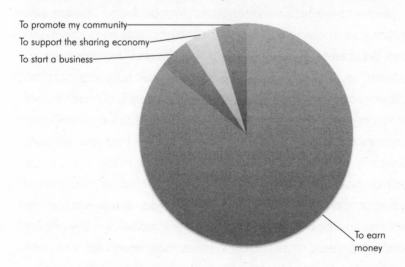

Many hosts believe that their homeshare is profitable, but they are actually running at a loss. This is because they have not accounted for all their expenses. If you are serious about making money from your homeshare, make sure you track all expenses. Under expenses, create categories for different costs including utility bills, laundry services, maintenance charges, management costs, advertising, and any other homeshare-related bills you receive. This will provide you with information to understand what the largest expenses for your business are and to see whether there are opportunities for expense reduction anywhere.

> We are happy to provide a fruit basket and a few amenities upon arrival, and replenish them in the case of longer stays. You have to manage the expenses associated with homesharing though . . . One guest took a liking to our personal supply of rare whisky!
>
> Howard, host from Hong Kong

Get into the habit of logging your income and tracking your expenses, and you'll avoid end-of-year accounting chaos and the stress of not knowing how your business is performing.

Tracking income and expenditure requires a certain discipline, but it is not difficult. Keep all receipts for goods and services purchased, and input these at least once a month into your book-keeping system. Divide your finances into either revenue or expenditure items. At the same time as recording revenue, keep records of your guests, including their names, contact details and booking information. Keep track of the money you have received for their stay, including deposits and any other paid services they have requested. Add separate categories to track extra income received from the booking fee, extra bed charges and any other guest fees. Keep the cleaning fee separate, as this may need to be adjusted later – for example, if guests leave the property in a state that requires an additional cleaning charge.

I live by myself in a large house. I was faced with the decision of selling my home or renting out the downstairs apartment to provide some income. I had a bad experience with a long-term rental, so when my son told me about Airbnb, I thought I would try it. That was three years ago and I've been busy ever since.

Ingrid, host from the United States

SAMPLE HOMESHARE PROFIT AND LOSS STATEMENT

REVENUE

		Assumptions
Base accommodation	15,000	*150/night for 100 nights*
Cleaning	3,200	*80 for 40 cleans*
Extra persons	600	*25/night for 30 extra person nights*
Additional services	400	*Additional cleaning for long stays*
Total Revenue	**19,200**	

EXPENSES

Direct Accommodation Expenses

Cleaning	3,200	*80 for 40 cleans*
Laundry	1,200	*30 for 40 transitions*
Booking fees	750	*5% of base accommodation*

Indirect Accommodation Expenses

Grounds and maintenance	2,240	*120/month gardener, 800 maintenance*
Supplies	1,200	*30 for 40 visits*
Utilities	2,300	*Electricity, water and gas*
Marketing	350	*Printed business cards and postcards*
General and administration	2,210	*Property taxes, council rates, insurance*
Total Expenses	**13,450**	

PROFIT	**5,750**
Profit Margin	30%

Most hosts will have to deal with a combination of paper and electronic receipts and invoices. We make most of our purchases and payments online, which avoids the need for keeping paper records. If you do have paper receipts, input them regularly and ensure you are not doubling up, as many service providers may also send a copy of their bill via email. As far as possible, we advise keeping all accounts and receipts online on a cloud service such as Dropbox. That way, you will never lose a receipt.

I started hosting to generate some revenue whilst on sabbatical and travelling for weeks/months at a time. Homesharing is a great way to supplement your income but like all things, it requires effort to be successful.

Helen, host from Australia

TIPS AND IDEAS
Open a homeshare bank account
Open a bank account solely for your homeshare business, with a credit card too if possible. Put everything through this account, and make homeshare-related payments only with this credit card. This will streamline your banking and create an easy-to-manage income and expenditure tracking system.

We set up a limited company to ensure I legally declare my rental income in the most tax efficient way possible, but this takes a lot of administrative time.

Ricci, host from Hong Kong and Malaysia

FORECASTING AND BUDGETING

Working out likely sales and how much managing the business will cost you can be a difficult task at any time, but particularly when you are starting out. Remember that this is not an exact science. Forecasting is a predictive exercise that involves making educated guesses about your income and expenditure. Nonetheless, it is a task worth doing if you want to set yourself realistic expectations of how busy you are going to be and how much money you can make for your efforts.

Start by developing a financial forecast for your business for the next three years. Base this on assumptions of anticipated revenue, calculated according to occupancy and pricing, and operating expenses. This forecast will give you a rough indication of the likely size of your business. Your projections should show increased revenue from one year to the next, as well as higher occupancy rates and increased nightly rates for each consecutive year, to show how your business will grow. If you are planning to start or increase spending on marketing and advertising, include these expenses too. Then develop a budget, a more detailed – and hopefully more accurate – revenue and expense projection for the first year, itemized by month.

The random nature of bookings is a big challenge and since it is our main income, there is a difficulty in knowing how to budget and control expenses.

Ricci, host from Hong Kong and Malaysia

THE BUSINESS PLAN

One way to structure this information is to write a business plan. Business plans are a valuable tool for the business owner. We recommend preparing a business plan because it will help you focus on what priorities and schedules are required to keep your business on track. While your bank or lender may want to see a business plan before they release funds, you should write it mainly for yourself with a view to being able to see how the business has fared after a year.

Include your aspirations and plans. What are your plans for your homeshare business? Are you seeking to achieve Airbnb Superhost status or another performance marker by the end of the year, or later? Have you made plans to hire a new cleaning team or a professional website designer to attract better reviews or more business? This is where you should lay out your plans and rationale.

Lessons learned can also be included in the business plan. For example, if part of the property suffered fire damage and the insurance cover was inadequate to meet the rebuilding costs, entering this experience in your business plan will serve to explain additional expenses as well as reminding you to insure your property adequately in the future.

Market changes that affect your business performance should also be included. Has a new backpacker hostel just opened opposite your homeshare? Has a new access road been completed that will help guests reach your homeshare more easily? Has a new entertainment venue opened that will attract more guests? Is there a new annual festival in your neighbourhood which will attract new guests?

Include them all in the plan to explain your revenue assumptions.

Your business plan should include:

- Your vision for the business – why are you running the homeshare?
- Financial and non-financial objectives, such as achieving a certain annual revenue, providing an alternative to backpacker accommodation, becoming an Airbnb Superhost.
- Your unique value proposition: What is special about your homeshare? What will attract guests?
- Financial projections. Develop a forecast spreadsheet that lays out your expected revenues and expenses for each of the next three years, and an annual action plan, or to-do list, that supports your key strategies, lists actions to take, due dates and responsibilities. Include your monthly revenue, expense and profit targets for the next 12 months.

The length of your business plan will vary according to the scale of your homeshare, your vision, and your experience of the business. A business plan can be anywhere from a one- to two-page outline to a comprehensive 100-page document that includes an overview of the industry, tourism facilities, analysis of competitor offerings, guest profiling and more. We advise keeping to the essentials rather than becoming bogged down in details. You can always revise and add to it later as your knowledge of the business grows. We spent three months writing our current 79-page business plan, working with a consultant from the hospitality industry, but only after the business had been up and running for three years.

Know your numbers

It pays to closely monitor the cost of every item and service, especially when you are starting out. If you are an absent host or are outsourcing part of the homeshare management to a third party, this becomes even more important, as we learned to our cost.

When assessing our financial performance after the second year of business, we were unpleasantly surprised to find that the expenses were significantly higher than planned. This led us to scrutinize all the expense items that had been provided by our management team, a real-estate agent. We found that the team, which was responsible for buying supplies for the property, had been adding an extra 10–20% to all the supply costs, which was not in the agreed contract.

It was an expensive but formative lesson. When we hired a new manager, we made sure to choose a team with an understanding of hospitality rather than real estate management – a very different business. We also knew their numbers much better. We were able to clarify with the new team exactly what was expected of them and how much it would cost. Together we defined precise roles and responsibilities for each step of the business, from calendar management, branding and marketing, to managing transitions, meeting and greeting guests, and carrying out renovations and maintenance. Each role and the tasks it entailed and standards expected were clearly laid out and agreed. This provided clarity and clear expectations on both sides.

We bought the house a couple of years ago for the extended family to use, but it was often vacant. When we happened across Airbnb, we decided to try it out in order to monetize the asset and it's been very successful.

Sidharth, host from India

ASSET MANAGEMENT

Big or small, your homeshare is full of assets. These comprise all the fixtures and fittings used by your guests. As a homeshare host, your assets are part of your business and need to be accounted for as well as taken care of.

You may think that you will remember every item provided in the homeshare, especially if you are living there, but over time it is easy to forget exactly what each room should contain, especially if you are an absent host. So the first step is to create an asset register – an inventory of every item. List what every item is, its location, description, replacement value, date and place of purchase, if available, and supplement with a photograph. Everything should be included, from the bedside rug and the curtains to the air-conditioning unit and the alarm clock, and from the toaster to the ironing board to the hairdryer. When listing electrical items such as televisions, include the manufacturer and model number to make repairs or replacement easier. Carry out the inventory on a room-by-room basis, and remember to include fixtures and fittings that are located outdoors, such as BBQs.

As well as helping you keep track of your homeshare's contents, the asset register will be useful in several other ways. In the event of breakage or theft, it will be invaluable as a record of the original contents of your homeshare. For financial management purposes, you will be able to use the register annually to calculate the depreciation of your assets, an expense item that will reduce your tax liability. On a regular basis, the asset register will help to remind you when maintenance is required, for example when the air-conditioning ventilators need to be cleaned. And on a day-to-day basis, the asset register will prove its worth as a checklist for your transition team, who can refer to it to help place items correctly in the room, and who should sign off on the accuracy of the contents after each transition.

CAPITAL MANAGEMENT

Capital management is the effective management of the capital you have invested in your homeshare, whether you are buying it specifically to use as a homeshare or converting your property or part of it for use as a homeshare. To manage your capital well, consider two key questions: how much do you want to invest in the property? And how much money do you need to spend on upgrading or maintaining it? It is important to make these calculations carefully at the outset to ensure that you don't overspend relative to the projected sale value and returns on your investment.

We can point to the example of our Sydney apartment, a small property which we bought three years ago and renovated from scratch to make it suitable for homeshare use, and from which to earn an income. At the outset, we worked out whether it made more financial sense to rent the apartment out on a long-term or short-term basis. After calculating that short-term rentals would earn two to three times the long-term rental rate, we opted for short-term lets. We started renovating only after working out how much we could expect to earn in short-term rental income and how much the renovation would cost. We estimated occupancy at about 60% at a certain nightly rate plus cleaning costs, as we knew that there was demand for accommodation in the apartment's location.

Every homeshare is different and this calculation will not work for all properties. Even for our own property, the figure we arrived at turned out to be inaccurate, though happily on the plus side: the occupancy rate is closer to 85%.

Making a similar calculation for your own business should take into account the location of your property. A small property centrally located in a global and popular city such as Sydney is likely to see higher occupancy than a more prestigious or larger property in a secondary city or an out-of-town location. Our Sydney apartment appeals to several different market segments – young couples, single travellers, business travellers – making higher occupancy more likely.

Over time, the income received from your homeshare business will increase the value of the property – your capital – as a property that realizes a high income will be more attractive to potential buyers or investors and makes a higher selling price more likely.

Summary

- Treat your homeshare as a business.

- Keep records of all revenue and expenses.

- Understand and fulfil your tax obligations.

- Open a bank account and a credit card solely for your homeshare business.

- Keep a list of guests and their contact details.

- Consider writing a business plan with a financial forecast and budget.

- Develop an asset registry.

- If you are considering buying a property to use as a homeshare, calculate the likely returns first to ensure its viability as an investment.

8

Reporting

Keeping records of your business is important, but it is even more critical to report and analyze this data. Reporting performance reveals how healthy your business is and also provides you with insights into how you can improve the business and forecast future results more accurately. Running a predictable business gives you peace of mind and the confidence to continually improve your homeshare operation, based on a clear picture of your actual performance.

Homeshare hosts who are serious about running a successful business should monitor four key performance indicators every month: occupancy, daily rate, guest reviews and profit. You can measure how well or badly your business is doing by comparing this data against the same results from the previous month or year, against your budget, or against competitor benchmarks.

Track your homeshare performance as if it was a business. We measure occupancy and daily rate each month, relative to the previous month as well as the same month last year.

Mitch, host from Australia

Key performance indicators to monitor

- **Occupancy:** refers to how many nights your home-share is booked relative to the number of nights available in a certain time period. Occupancy not only shows the impact of past sales and market-ing performance, but also identifies future opportunities.
- **Daily rate:** the average daily rate charged for your homeshare. This measure aggregates any peak rates and discounts offered to show your average revenue per night sold.
- **Guest review ratings:** guest reviews measure your level of customer service and are critical for encourag-ing future bookings. They provide feedback on the guest experience and the quality of the homeshare, and help forecast future bookings.
- **Profit:** indicates the financial viability of your business. Tracking profitability is critical to ensuring that your business is viable, and that you are not spending more than you earn.

OCCUPANCY

Knowing how frequently your homeshare is booked helps you assess past sales and marketing performance and identify future opportunities. Optimizing your occupancy rates is the key to any successful accommodation business. Occupancy is a percentage that is calculated by dividing the number of booked nights by the number of available nights in a certain time period. For example, if you have guests staying for 10 nights in a 30-day month, then your occupancy is 33% for that month.

Occupancy (%) = number of nights sold / total number of available nights in a period

Tracking occupancy allows hosts to assess the potential for future bookings and to work out how many nights have been 'lost' because of no guest bookings. Remember, nights at your homeshare are a perishable item; an empty homeshare night can never be recovered and represents missed revenue.

Occupancy is also a measure of the success of your sales and marketing strategies. Achieving high occupancy means you are doing a great job of building awareness about your homeshare and attracting guests. It means potential guests are able to find your property and believe that your prices are reasonable, so they want to stay. If you have low occupancy, then you should examine your sales or marketing strategies in order to reach more potential guests, generate more enquiries and improve your enquiry-to-booking conversion rate.

Highs and lows of occupancy rates

No magic formula exists for establishing what 'high occupancy' is. It will vary depending on your property, its location and its competitors. In the Blue Mountains, many homeshares operate at an annual occupancy rate of 30%, as the Blue Mountains is an area popular for weekend visitors from Sydney. The 30% rate is based on the assumption that most weekends and school holiday periods will be booked in a given year, but that otherwise the homeshare is likely to be empty. However, for our Sydney apartment, which is in an urban setting and is ideal for business travellers and overseas or interstate guests, we expect occupancy of at least 80%.

Establish a rough benchmark for your property by researching your competitors' occupancy rates and setting yourself a similar target.

DAILY RATE

Knowing your average daily rate is important when reviewing whether your pricing needs to be increased or decreased to drive further business.

Daily rate ($/£) =
total revenue / nights sold for a specific period

If you are in the habit of discounting, you may be surprised that your average daily rate is significantly lower than your advertised rate. On the other hand, if you have successfully sold many peak-rate nights, then your average daily rate may be higher than you had assumed. Your average daily rate is an important data point to be used when comparing your rates to those of your competitors. If your average daily rate appears to be lower than that of competitors, then it may be possible to increase your rates without reducing the number of sales you make.

The average daily rate, when combined with your occupancy, also drives a commonly used hotel industry metric called revenue per available day, or RevPAD. This measure may be one which you choose to track.

Revenue per available day or RevPAD ($/£) =
occupancy × average daily rate

MEASURING GUEST REVIEWS

Guest reviews provide valuable feedback on how guests are actually experiencing your property and the quality of your homeshare, as well as helping to forecast future bookings. Feedback is given through ratings and comments, both written and spoken. The actual ratings and the frequency of guest reviews are also a valuable source of information about the health of your business.

It is worth spending time each month analyzing the feedback received from your guests. Every business learns by listening to its customers, and a homeshare business is no different. If your guest reviews are positive, keep doing what you are doing, remembering that there is always room for improvement. But if your reviews are weaker than those received by your competitors, consider making changes to your guest experience based on the feedback you have received.

The way you measure guest reviews will depend on which online travel agencies you use. For example, Airbnb's 1 to 5 star rating scale is easy to track, and the Airbnb Superhost status is another marker. TripAdvisor has a similar rating system, and offers awards based on targets that hosts can aspire to reach. Tally the number of stars your homeshare receives and calculate the average for the month. Make sure that you also take account of guests' qualitative comments when reviewing your guest feedback.

MEASURING PROFITABILITY

Measuring the money that you are making is critical to ensuring that the business is viable by verifying that you are earning more than you spend. Calculate the profitability of your homeshare by subtracting the total expenses from total revenue for a certain period. If the result is positive, you are financially viable; if the result is negative, then your business is losing money. This will be for one of two reasons: either you have not achieved high enough revenue, or your expenses are too high.

> *At first, we were just curious to see if anyone would rent, as our Croatian village is rather small and off the beaten track. We looked at our costs to drive back and forth from Sweden (tolls, food, lodging, etc.) and thought that if we could cover our costs that would be great. And in fact, homesharing does now cover all of these costs.*
>
> Tom, host from Croatia and Sweden

You can also measure the profit margin of your business to give you a better insight into the state of the business. This figure allows you to see what percentage of your income is profit. To calculate your profit margin, divide your profit by your revenue.

The level of profitability of your business should not come as a surprise to you. If you have prepared a budget that identifies expenses and estimated revenue, then you should already have an idea of your profit margin.

Profit ($/£) = revenue minus expenses
Profit margin (%) = profit / revenue

Profit should be measured at the end of each month. Results will vary from month to month, so allow at least six months before expecting to see a pattern. Remember that peak periods will emerge, so a highly profitable month may not occur again for another year.

Some hosts knowingly run unprofitable homeshare businesses because they believe that the capital growth provided by the property is adequate return, or because they love meeting guests and enjoy the role of being a host and do not need to make money.

If you want to make your business commercially successful, aim for 15–20% profitability. This should include the cost of the host's own time. For example, if you spend three hours per guest visit on making the booking, communicating with guests, overseeing the transition and welcoming them, this time should be costed and included in your total expenses, even if you are not actually paying yourself a salary. The discipline of including this cost allows you to understand the true financial position of the business and will provide useful information for a future investor or purchaser.

> *For an investment property, you should make twice as much with homeshare than if you were renting long-term.*
>
> Mitch, host from Australia

BENCHMARKING PERFORMANCE

When you start out, benchmark your homeshare's performance against your past results, from month to month. What you would like to see is an increase in occupancy, guest ratings and profit, from month to month. Over time, you can track your results relative to the same month in the previous year. This will provide you with trends that indicate the high and low seasons for your business.

You can also benchmark your homeshare relative to your competitors. This will give you a true indication of how your business is doing in market terms. To do this, first identify who your competitors are. An ideal comparison is with properties that are similar in size to yours, are targeting similar prospective guests and are located in the same neighbourhood. Arrange to either speak to these hosts if you know them, or obtain their performance data from online sources. Hosts are usually very happy to discuss their business, especially if you meet them at host community functions or you have friends who are running homeshares.

Don't be surprised, however, if other hosts are not familiar with their own business results. Many hosts track their pricing, daily rates and guest review status, but not their occupancy levels or profitability.

TIPS AND IDEAS
Comparing apples and oranges
Avoid benchmarking your results against homeshares in different locations, or in places with different demands. For example, after a concerted marketing effort, Dantosa Blue Mountains Retreat now has occupancy of over 60%, while the Sydney apartment – which is listed on only one online travel agency – has occupancy of over 85%. However, the profit margin is approximately 50% for Dantosa and only 35% for the Sydney apartment. These metrics highlight the difference in the two homeshares: one is large and in a predominantly weekend visitor area; the other is small and in an urban environment, close to the central business district.

MANAGEMENT SCORECARD

A management scorecard is a summary of how your business is going. It contains a record of your results for each key performance indicator, relative to your budget, and the previous month's results, or another benchmark, such as your competitors' average performance. Prepare your own management scorecards, at least initially. It is a good discipline and helps you become very familiar with your own numbers. Over time, if you have delegated the responsibility for managing your homeshare to someone else, you may ask them to prepare regular reports for your review.

Homestay Monthly Scorecard

	This Month	Last Month	Budget
Occupancy	55%	45%	48%
Daily Rate	59	61	63
Guest Reviews	★★★★	★★★	★★★★★
Profit Margin	18%	9%	20%
Expenses	$750	$780	$780
Revenue	$920	$860	$980
Profit	$170	$80	$200

In the example above, it is clear that the results for this homeshare have improved since the previous month, however guest ratings and revenue are not as high as the budget set.

OPERATIONS REPORTING

For hosts who outsource any element of their operations, it is important to obtain regular operations reports from your transition team or manager, as well as reports on key performance indicators. How are your transition cleans going? Are you managing expenses in accordance with your budget? How long does a standard clean take at your homeshare? What maintenance is required at your property in the next six months? Are your instructions regarding presentation of the property being carried out every time? Have the scheduled repairs been conducted as planned? Has an accurate list of supplies required for next month been compiled?

We hold a monthly operations call with our Dantosa transition manager. The main purpose of this call is to review feedback, discuss upcoming bookings and guest requirements, review maintenance and spring-cleaning activities, confirm requirements for supplies, and confirm status of specific action items, such as buying new linen. A sample agenda for your maintenance call is shown on the following page.

ADDITIONAL MANAGEMENT REPORTING

To gain a deeper understanding of your business, you may choose to measure other, more sophisticated key performance indicators as well as occupancy, daily rate, guest reviews and profit. In particular, it is worth understanding your enquiry-to-booking conversion rate for each enquiry source, as well as revenue per available day. Managing the line items in your profit and loss statement is also important, relative to the budget you have set, as well as your last year of operation.

dantosa
blue mountains retreat

Agenda
Operations Call

---

6 September 2016

1. General Update
- Feedback from guests
- Feedback from transition team

2. Dantosa Operations
- Review upcoming bookings
- Review upcoming tours
- Review list of maintenance items
- Confirm requirements for new supplies
- Confirm dates for next spring clean

3. Dantosa Management
- Update on productivity improvements
- Agenda for upcoming visit

4. Other items
- See list of action items and review status

Unless you are simply letting out a small room, you cannot do it all yourself. Websites, publicity and marketing, enquiries, preparing the homeshare, refurbishing, receiving guests, endeavouring to provide a good holiday experience, entertaining great guests and suffering imbeciles, cleaning and maintenance, being a tour guide, assessing sales channels for return on investment, handling finances and pricing. And all of these variable elements require costing into your price – a price that must also remain competitive. Homesharing is a complex business, and we need to treat it as such.

Derrick, host from Thailand

The key performance indicators in the following table are relevant for any homeshare property, but typically only larger operators measure them all. They offer further insight into how your business is working and what performance patterns are appearing. You may choose to measure these additional key performance indicators less frequently than your standard monthly reporting.

Additional Homeshare Key Performance Indicators

Additional Key Performance Indicators	Calculation	Reason for Measurement
Conversion rate (%)	Number of sales / number of enquiries	Sales strategy and approach
Conversion rate by enquiry source (%)	Conversion rate for each source of enquiry, e.g. website, Airbnb, email campaign, referral	Sales, marketing
Lead time (number of days)	Average time booking made before the visit	Pricing, forecasting
Revenue per available day or RevPAD ($/£)	Revenue / total number of available nights	Forecasting
Average revenue per visit ($/£)	Revenue / number of visits	Forecasting
Sales pipeline ($/£)	Future revenue sold for next 12 months	Forecasting
On-time complete transitions (%)	Number of on-time and high-quality transitions / total number of transitions	Transitions quality
Cleanliness rating (number of stars)	Average online travel agency rating on cleanliness	Transitions quality
Guests who leave reviews (%)	Number of reviews / total number of visits	Review process
Guests per booking	Total number of guests / number of bookings	Forecasting
Extra guests per booking	Total number of extra guests / number of bookings	Forecasting
Length of stay (number of days)	Total number of days stayed / number of bookings	Forecasting, pricing
Repeat guests (%)	Repeat guests / total number of guests	Marketing
Effectiveness of marketing activity	e.g. Facebook likes, website hits, return on investment on marketing investments, newsletter open rate	Marketing
Metrics specific to your online travel agency	e.g. Airbnb Superhost, TripAdvisor awards, listing ranking	Sales, marketing

INVESTMENT IN HOMESHARE

There is now literature and research available to assist investors who are purchasing properties with the intention of using them solely for homeshare. It is essential to research all aspects on purchasing such property carefully. One writer for the data analytics service AirDNA, Tom Caton, talks of the six steps of Airbnb property investing as:

- Find a location using Airdna data analytics.
- Work out the regulations.
- Zero in on an individual property.
- Account for *all* of the costs.
- Factor in house price appreciation.
- Understand *exact* expected returns on your investment.

AUTOMATED REPORTING AND MANAGEMENT TOOLS

The business of homesharing is developing fast. Advice forums, websites, master classes and Facebook pages are popping up, offering help on how to start your homeshare business. Many of these sites and forums are great and certainly worth signing up for to learn more about homeshare. One of the major challenges is that as competition for homeshare properties grow, in particular in major urban centres, standing out from the crowd and ensuring your property is seen by as many potential guests as possible becomes the major strategic challenge.

To improve your occupancy and your revenue, you need distribution. Over time this means listing on multiple sites and optimizing the number of online travel agencies with which you are listed to attract more potential guests. Knowing your target guest market is important, as is understanding which sites target that desired market. As your business grows, having a well-oiled administrative machine is essential to manage multiple booking calendars, to account for the revenues and expenses of your operation, to implement your cleaning transitions on time and at the required quality standard, to streamline your own website, and to follow up guests for feedback (and, hopefully, 5 star reviews).

We assume that over the coming years, the homeshare industry can expect an integrated technology solution designed specifically for hosts to manage their business from end to end. This software would aggregate data from multiple online travel agencies and provide one calendar, as well as useful management reports with insights into the homeshare's performance. For now, the homeshare industry is left with cobbling together different applications with which to manage their business; this means operating at scale is a complex exercise which often has to be done manually. After selecting your online travel agencies, some of the technology solutions which are currently available to build an end-to-end, automated business system include:

- Accounting (creating your revenue and expense reports and syncing with your bank account): XERO, Quickbooks, Sage One, MYOB
- Channel manager (syncing booking calendars, pricing and availability): Beds24, Kigo, Guesty, Bookingsync, Barefoot, Xotelia, Tokeet
- Analysis and reporting (monitoring business performance by delivering key data from many sources to a single dashboard): Databox, iDashboards, Grow, Segment
- Integration and automation (helps non-technical people connect apps and services they use and carry out

automated functions or workflows): Zapier, Atlassian, Trello (owned by Atlassian), IFTTT, Podio

- Cleaning and transition management (managing cleaners and cleaning transitions): GetProperly
- Pricing management (monitoring pricing of competitors): Beyond Pricing, Price Method, Airbnb's Smart Pricing, Everbooked, AirDNA.

In order to make the administration more efficient, less hands on, and to maximize revenue we have started using BEDS24 for channel management, XERO for accounting, Databox for analysis/reporting and Zapier for integration and automation.

Ricci, host from Hong Kong and Malaysia

Summary

- Don't neglect reporting. Tracking the performance of your homeshare helps you identify opportunities to improve your business.

- Review occupancy, daily rate, guest reviews and profit on a monthly basis.

- Manage the line items in your profit and loss statement, relative to your budget.

- Talk to other hosts to assess how your business is doing compared to similar homeshares.

- As your homeshare business matures, consider measuring additional key performance indicators such as conversion rate and revenue per available day.

9

Driving Business

Once you have regular management reports for your home-share business, you need to analyze your results and decide whether any changes are needed. The results of key performance indicators can act as red flags.

Would you like higher occupancy? If occupancy is low, your daily rate may be too high, dissuading guests from staying with you. How are your guest reviews? If guest reviews are poor, take note of the feedback and make the necessary changes. Perhaps your listing description is not accurate, your homeshare is not clean enough, or you have not provided the basic supplies that guests expect. Are you happy with your current profit? If your expenses exceed your revenue, this means that your business is unprofitable. You may be spending too much on supplies. Are you offering a five-star experience with luxury soaps, fruit baskets, chocolates and wine, for the price of two-star accommodation? If so, it is time to rethink the level of the guest experience you want to provide and the associated expenses.

Profitability of a homeshare business is a challenge, particularly dealing with the ups and downs of month-to-month revenue and offsetting the maintenance costs associated with an apartment in an older building.

Ricci, host from Hong Kong and Malaysia

FIVE LEVERS TO DRIVE YOUR BUSINESS

If there is room for improvement, you can drive business by using five key levers: marketing, sales, guest experience, transitions and management. More marketing activity and targeted campaigns will increase awareness of your homeshare to potential guests. Increasing the efficiency of your sales procedures and better pricing should result in more sales and more revenue per booking. Making the changes recommended by guests should enhance the guest experience and lead to better guest reviews and more repeat visits. Improving the quality and speed of your transitions, as well as lowering the cost of transitions, will make your business more successful. Managing your homeshare strategically by implementing disciplined business planning, workable policies and risk management procedures, and careful expense management will build a sustainable foundation for your business and give it the best possible chance for growth.

> *Your total annual revenue from homeshare should be at least 10% of your property's purchase price.*
>
> Mitch, host from Australia

The table opposite summarizes ways to improve the results of your top key performance indicators and to strengthen your overall business.

Impact of Levers

● high ◐ medium ○ low impact		Impact on Key Performance Indicator			
Lever	**Action**	**Occu-pancy**	**Daily Rate**	**Guest Reviews**	**Profit**
Marketing	Enhance your unique value proposition (key marketing message), including reviewing your offer (is your homeshare business-ready or pet-friendly?) and update listings	●	◐	●	◐
	Strengthen your homeshare brand (name, photographs)	◐	◐	●	◐
	Review current online travel agencies and consider adding new ones	●	◐	○	◐
	Establish a social media presence (Facebook, Instagram, etc.)	◐	○	◐	◐
	Build a website with appropriate search engine optimization so potential guests find you	◐	○	○	◐
	Run direct marketing campaigns (email to your past clients and contacts)	◐	○	○	◐
	Offer print-based marketing materials (post-cards, brochures)	◐	○	○	◐
	Consider paid advertising (online, maga-zines, newspapers, cinema, radio) aimed at specific audience groups	●	○	◐	◐
Sales	Be more responsive to enquiries (e.g. set a target of response within one hour)	●	○	●	●
	Refine tone of communications and develop standard templates	◐	○	◐	○
	Review current pricing, introduce more sophisticated pricing by day/date/season	◐	●	○	●
	Introduce upsales opportunities (e.g. addi-tional services, late check-out fee)	◐	◐	◐	●
Guest Experience	Make improvements to presentation of prop-erty (e.g. paint internal walls, linen quality, declutter)	◐	◐	●	◐
	Add new equipment and supplies for your guests (e.g. rice cooker, luxury bath salts)	◐	◐	●	◐
	Introduce services for your guests (e.g. babysitting, massage, chef)	◐	○	●	◐
	Add more of a personal touch during guest stays (e.g. in person meet-and-greet, phone call mid-stay, 'concierge' services)	◐	◐	●	◐
Transitions	Make improvements to your processes to ensure consistently high-quality transitions	○	○	●	◐
	Improve the efficiency of transitions	◐	○	○	◐
	Reduce the total cost of transitions	○	○	○	●
Management	Manage your home stay strategically (vision, budget, policies, awareness of industry trends and competitors)	●	◐	◐	●
	Provide strong operational oversight with effective processes and back-up procedures	○	○	◐	●

MARKETING: BUILDING ON THE BASICS

Marketing offers a wide variety of solutions to increase your business, and many of them cost nothing but your time. Successful marketing ensures that potential guests find you. Basic marketing involves defining your unique value proposition, establishing a brand for your homeshare by using professional photographs and giving your property a name, and listing your homeshare on at least one online travel agency. If you have done all of this and you are still concerned that your homeshare does not have a strong enough profile, then assess the effectiveness of your current marketing before considering any further steps. Ask yourself:

- Does your unique value proposition resonate with potential guests? Can it be improved, or has it in fact changed? Consider redefining and rewriting this key marketing message to reflect the best that your homeshare has to offer.
- Have you built a brand for your homeshare? Does it have a personality that can be shared through its name and presentation?
- Are your photographs as good as they can be? Do they offer a complete picture of your homeshare? Should you add more photographs to showcase new features or equipment in your homeshare?
- Is your listing description complete or does it need more information, based on the questions you receive from guests? Consider updating your own host profile too, with a more recent photograph or more information about yourself now that you are a more experienced host. Mention your passion for hosting and why you enjoy being a homeshare host.

- Are your policies appropriate for your potential guests? For example, if your minimum length of stay is three days, you may be excluding weekend visitors. Should you reconsider allowing pets at your property? This could attract a large number of guests who would otherwise go elsewhere. Make the most of the descriptors provided by your online travel agency, such as Airbnb's Business Ready criteria which points business travellers to specific homeshares.
- Are you satisfied that your current online travel agency selection is working for you? Do you have a strong conversion rate from enquiries to sales? Consider listing on additional sites that may be more appealing to your target audience. Remember to look for sites with broad reach (for example, Airbnb, HomeAway, Stayz in Australia, TripAdvisor, VRBO, Booking.com) and strong brands that are directed towards your target audience (including the correct language support). Consider listing on niche online travel agents, for example, luxury sites such as OneFineStay.

ADVANCED MARKETING

Once you have assured yourself that your basic marketing approach is functioning as well as possible, consider using more sophisticated marketing strategies to increase your sales.

One option to drive additional business is to expand the way you currently market or advertise your homeshare. Spend time on online social marketing websites, for example by setting up a Facebook page or an Instagram account for your business. You can also create or develop your own website. Paid options including printing and distributing brochures or postcards, paying for advertisements in local newspapers, on tourist websites, in tourist magazines, on radio, or in cinemas. You can be as creative and daring as you wish, but before committing to additional marketing, set a budget for any paid marketing activities. You can also try direct marketing to past guests, by emailing them with a special offer for particular nights you want to sell.

Remember that every night your homeshare is empty is a missed opportunity for you to make money; unsold nights are a perishable item, lost for ever. Targeted marketing aims to sell visits to your homeshare that would otherwise be lost. The idea is to identify a target audience – the type of guest you want to attract and to whom you will direct your advertising – and then work out the best channels to reach them. Are they business travellers, retirees who could play golf at your local course, or international guests who would appreciate marketing materials written in their own language? What is the profile of the tourists who mainly visit your neighbourhood? Are they young visitors who like to connect with your property online? Are they older and more likely to read print-based material, such as newspapers and magazines? Are they likely to respond to an email from you, or would they be annoyed to receive a marketing email?

Seven steps to successful targeted marketing

1. Define your target audience.
2. Identify the channels that are most appropriate for reaching the target audience, such as social media, radio advertising, special interest magazines, emails, brochures.
3. Estimate the costs of marketing in these channels.

4. Identify opportunities to enhance your homeshare to appeal to your target groups. For example, consider providing baby equipment, obtaining Business Ready accreditation via Airbnb, or providing pet-friendly options.

5. Review your wish-list of marketing channels. Based on your available budget, select the most appropriate marketing initiatives and plan a suitable schedule for your campaign.

6. Prepare your marketing materials including a tagline or key message, as well as graphic design and printing specifications.

7. Implement your marketing campaign and keep track of the effectiveness of each individual marketing activity.

Once you have launched your campaign, be sure to ask enquirers where they heard about your homeshare and track the source of the enquiry. At the end of your campaign, use this information to assess which marketing strategy was the most effective, so you can replicate it in the future.

TIPS AND IDEAS
Make every day Valentine's Day

If your occupancy during the week is high because of business travellers, try targeting local couples for staycations at your homeshare on the weekends. Target both young and old couples who want to indulge in a break in their own city. If they are young, they are likely to respond better to advertising via online channels. If they are elderly, you may get a better response from a flyer sent to their home. Design a weekend-away-from-home offer, including a bottle of champagne and luxury bath products. Advertise it on your website, on your Facebook page and on Instagram, or with a beautifully designed postcard to drop in people's letterboxes. You can also send the same information to all your past guests by email.

Track your revenue as a result of this marketing campaign. You will probably find that one weekend sale covers the entire costs of your campaign, making it a very worthwhile exercise.

TIPS AND IDEAS
Make an impact online

If you have a website, analyze how much traffic it receives. To increase the number of hits, consider using search engine optimization tools. These include identifying the best key words to describe your homeshare and, in particular, to highlight what is unique about your property. You then need to ensure that these words are repeated frequently in the content of your website. Some search engines, such as Google, offer paid options to have your website appear high on the list when someone searches for one of these words.

TARGETED MARKETING AT DANTOSA

To drive occupancy and profit at Dantosa, we embarked on an adventurous targeted marketing programme in our fourth year of operation. In the first years of operation, occupancy at Dantosa was high only at weekends and during school holidays, as its location in the Blue Mountains was mainly seen as a weekend getaway destination from Sydney. Deciding to try to increase the number of midweek visits to Dantosa, we identified three target audiences who could visit midweek: overseas visitors, retirees and small corporate groups. We decided to spend 10% of our budgeted annual revenue on targeted marketing activities, and created a marketing campaign to use for ads in an airline magazine and its associated travel website, postcards and 15-second video advertisements for cinema audiences. As part of the deal with the airline magazine, we invited the editor to stay at Dantosa to experience the property. At the same time, we upgraded the Dantosa website and created downloadable fact sheets aimed at the three target groups. We became more active on Facebook and regularly posted new photos aimed at the three groups. By joining a local chamber of commerce, we secured a slot on a local radio business show to talk about the homeshare industry and Dantosa. The table on page 146 summarizes the marketing channels we used.

We welcome diversity, and have had many who stay with us who have been rejected elsewhere because of their colour. Our listing states: 'We are proud to share that we will not discriminate against potential guests based on gender identity or expression, sexual orientation, religion, race/colour/ethnicity, national origin, age, marital or disability status. If you are respectful and we feel we can provide you with a great experience, we will happily host you!'

Megan, host from the United States

Dantosa Marketing Channels – 2016 Campaign

Target Audiences	Marketing Channels					
	Cinema	Airline	Facebook	Instagram	Newsletter	Website
Corporate	✓	✓				✓
Start-ups	✓	✓	✓	✓		✓
Retirees	✓	✓			✓	✓
Special interest groups	✓	✓				✓
International visitors		✓	✓	✓		✓
Chinese travellers		✓		✓		✓
Reunion	✓	✓	✓	✓	✓	✓
Small events		✓	✓	✓		✓
Repeat guests	✓	✓	✓	✓	✓	✓
Pink market	✓	✓	✓	✓		✓
Local businesses	✓		✓	✓		✓

This targeted marketing has successfully increased occupancy at Dantosa to over 60%. As a result of these campaigns, the number of enquiries rose by 15% and the number of corporate bookings more than doubled. Additionally the nature of the enquiries changed; those received at the Dantosa website increased from 5% to 30% of the total number. This was a positive outcome, as the conversion rate of enquiries-to-bookings on the website is 40%, significantly higher than on online travel agencies.

If you want to increase your marketing activity and know how to do it, then it is a good idea to do it yourself. Hiring professionals is likely to achieve a better result, but it will cost you money, so don't rush into this without careful planning.

For the Dantosa campaigns, we hired a creative director and a graphic designer to create the advertisements for the inflight magazine and travel website, but we liaised directly with the editors and marketing departments ourselves to reduce the overall costs.

MEASURING THE IMPACT OF TARGETED MARKETING

Make sure that you have a way to measure the effectiveness of any targeted marketing that you conduct. The easiest way is to track the source of each enquiry by asking the enquirer where they heard about you and keep a record. Each month, track the number of enquiries, the number of sales and the revenue associated with every source of enquiry. Compare these with your normal number of enquiries, sales and revenue at times when you have not been conducting targeted marketing campaigns. In this way, you can assess whether the additional marketing efforts and spend have been worthwhile.

Depending on the success of a specific marketing campaign, you may want to consider repeating it. This will depend on your occupancy – do you still need to fill the specific dates related to your campaign?

SALES

The homeshare industry is undoubtedly becoming more professional and more competitive, so it is important for hosts to focus on effective sales techniques. An example of this professionalization is homeshare occupancy in the United States, which grew from an average of 11 nights sold per month to 23 days, in 2016 alone.*

Your approach to sales directly impacts your bottom line. If your profit and occupancy results are not as strong as you would like, then it is worth examining your sales management. Four factors are critical to success in sales: being responsive to enquiries, speaking the same language as your potential guest by using an appropriate tone in communications, refining your pricing and upselling additional services.

> When I get an enquiry, I'm on to it straight away because they might be talking to other hosts. I usually respond within the hour, unless the enquiry comes after 11 p.m., in which case I answer them in the morning. My Airbnb response rate is 100%.
>
> James, host from Australia

How quickly do you respond to enquiries about your home-share? The best hosts guarantee a response within one hour. This shows potential guests that the host runs a professional operation and is likely to be reliable and to continue to be responsive – all great predictors of a good guest experience. If your conversion rate from enquiry to sale is less than 20%, start by reviewing how you communicate with prospective guests. The tone of your communications is very important and so is the medium you use for communication. If possible, call the enquirer – a phone call is a very effective way of communicating, as you can respond quickly to any questions the person may have about your homeshare and you can

* Source: AirDNA, 2017.

develop a friendly rapport with them during the conversation. When we decided to call enquirers, our conversion rate improved dramatically. We also found we were spending less time answering enquiries than when we responded by email.

> *Remember that your time is valuable – set your prices accordingly. I use an online pricing tool (Beyond Pricing) to make sure that I'm maximizing the income from my home.*
>
> Isaiah, host from the United States

TIPS AND IDEAS
Efficient but friendly communications

When writing an email to a prospective guest, keep it short and simple and make sure that you answer all their questions in an efficient but friendly way. Many enquirers decide not to proceed with a booking if they do not like the reply they receive. Always check the email for errors before you press 'send'.

Next, consider whether changing your pricing can improve your profit. Ask yourself how much you can increase your daily rate without damaging your ability to make a sale. If your occupancy is high and neighbouring competitors are charging a higher rate per night, you may want to consider raising your prices. When we first advertised our Sydney apartment on Airbnb, we set a low daily rate to encourage guests and to ensure that they received value for their money. Over time, once we were confident that there was a demand for the homeshare and we had a clearer understanding of our competitors' rates, we increased the prices. If your occupancy is low and you receive poor review ratings for 'value', then your prices may be too high and you can consider reducing them. This may lead to higher occupancy, which will in time increase your profit.

Hotels hire expert analysts to set their daily rates and these daily rates vary according to season, day of the week and the particular date. Hotel daily rates also vary according to how soon the booking will be made. This pricing expertize is diffi-cult to replicate for homeshares, but many online travel agen-cies allow hosts to vary their prices for different dates. With experience, you can try experimenting with your pricing. Start by identifying your peak and low periods – which days or times of year are you most likely to fill? Those dates should have the highest daily rates. When is your low season? Try reducing your daily rate for that period to encourage more bookings.

At Dantosa, the Easter weekend, long weekends and the July school holidays are peak times, as are all weekends during the winter months. The daily rates for those dates are 30–50% higher than they are for other periods. It took us some time to work out that guests expect this and will not be surprised or shocked at the higher rates.

Another way to increase profitability is to sell more to your confirmed guests. Are there additional services you can tempt them with, on which you can make a commission? Can you charge guests for a late check-out? These additional revenue streams may seem small, but they are profitable and will add up over time. At Dantosa, guests are offered optional extras such as local chefs who will come and cook for them, wine tastings run by a local winemaker, and massages. For each of these services, Dantosa charges a small commission. These additional charges now comprise 10% of the property's total revenue.

GUEST EXPERIENCE

Enhancing your guest experience is a great way to improve your reviews, as well as your occupancy. Take time to read your guest reviews and summarize the key themes. Then assess the viability of implementing the changes suggested. If all your guests complain about the quality of your towels, it is probably time to replace them with towels of higher quality. However, if just one guest requests the addition of an expensive new appliance, consider whether the investment is worthwhile.

Once you have made the improvements, make sure that you communicate them by updating your listing description and describing them on your website. When new coffee machines were installed at Dantosa, pictures of them were posted on Facebook. This showed past guests that we had listened to their recommendation, and also demonstrated to prospective guests that the Dantosa hosts are serious about continuous improvement.

Other ways to show you are committed to providing a wonderful guest experience are to take note of what your competitors offer their guests, and to follow advice that is offered by your online travel agency.

TRANSITIONS

Well-managed transitions between guests affect the success of your business. Not only can you sell more nights with confidence that your homeshare will be ready for the new guests, but the guest experience is enhanced by a well-presented property. If your guest reviews have not given you a five-star rating for cleanliness, then you should examine your transition procedures. You need to ensure that your homeshare is always well cleaned and fully prepared for the next guests. Do you need to find a new cleaner? Who is signing off that your homeshare is ready for the next guest and are they doing a wonderful job?

The cost of transitions may be the largest expense for your business, so it is important to manage that cost carefully. Can the clean be done quicker, while maintaining the same high quality? Would it make sense for you to manage some transitions yourself, rather than pay others to perform the job? Regularly reviewing the transition process and costs is an essential part of running a successful homeshare business. Spend time with other hosts to learn how they have improved their transition processes. Local hosts can be a source of valuable tips, such as recommended cleaners.

MANAGEMENT

Ultimately, the responsibility for the health of a homeshare business rests with its owner or host. It is the host who needs to manage the homeshare as a business. When looking at ways to drive business, you will need to think both strategically and operationally. From a strategic standpoint, ask yourself the following questions: What is the big picture for your homeshare business? Where do you want your business to be in three years' time? What size operation will you be running then and what kind of support team will you need to run it? What is the competitive landscape? Are other hosts in your area making changes that could leave you behind? Are you keeping up to date with the latest trends in hosting, for example hosting guests from mainland China? Having a clear vision and strategy will help you make the best decisions for your business and will improve your occupancy, guest reviews and profit.

Operationally, the host needs to ensure that the homeshare is managed using effective and efficient processes. This includes all aspects of the business, from marketing and sales, to presentation and the guest experience, to transitions and guest reviews, to financial and risk management. If the wheels are well-oiled, then your vehicle will run seamlessly.

Summary

To drive further business, consider the following actions:

- Increase your marketing activity (build a website, add a Facebook page, open an Instagram account, send email offers to past guests, pay for advertisements, list your property on additional online travel agencies).

- Modify your sales approach (be faster in answering enquiries, introduce more competitive pricing, add new revenue streams which are likely to be profitable).

- Enhance the guest experience (make the changes recommended by guests and advertise the improvements, ensure you manage guest expectations).

- Improve the quality and speed of transitions.

- Manage your business both strategically and operationally to ensure that your policies make sense, your expenses are managed, and your processes are effective. Pay attention to advice from online travel agencies and ensure your budget allows for improvements to your business.

Conclusion

This book has attempted to help you launch or improve your homeshare business, taking an incremental, step-by-step approach – from taking the plunge of advertising your property online to upgrading your financial management systems. We have aimed to show that every part of the homeshare business can be mastered by those with no professional experience. The most important prerequisites are a mindset of aiming for excellence and an appetite for hard work, learning and perseverance. We hope you have been inspired by finding that there are proven paths that you can follow if you want to build a successful, rewarding and profitable homeshare business.

If you have read this far, you will have realized that this book is only the start of the journey. Like every part of the hospitality business, the world of homesharing is constantly evolving and guests expect hosts to keep up with the latest trends and improvements. Running a successful homeshare business means never being complacent about your achievements. You will always be looking for ways to improve, to refine and to learn. That constant striving is what makes this business so interesting and rewarding.

The experiences we have shared in this book are complemented by HomeShare Solutions, an online service we run for homeshare hosts. This subscription-based website gives hosts more detailed information about every aspect of running a homeshare, along with checklists and tools to help you cover just about every scenario you are likely to face as a host. You will also be able to access case studies of hosts who share their experiences and the lessons they have learned, creating an invaluable resource for hosts both new and experienced. HomeShare Solutions subscribers can also join our online homeshare host community forum and access advisory services.

Please visit homesharesolutions.com to find out more.

Appendices

A. HOST PROFILES

This section provides information on the hosts who have provided input to this book and whose comments are included in earlier chapters. We deliberately selected a variety of hosts from around the world, each with a different homeshare story. Some are remote hosts who manage their homeshare properties from afar, some have various properties, some luxurious properties, others more modest ones, and some share their own homes with guests. These hosts use a variety of online travel agents to promote their homeshare listings; many are listed on Airbnb, but some hosts have developed their own websites, and others advertise on multiple platforms including Booking.com, TripAdvisor, HomeAway, OneFineStay and MisterB&B. These hosts are passionate about what they do and willingly agreed to be interviewed for this book. We hope that by reading their stories, you can identify with some of them and learn more about how best to manage your homeshare.

THE HOME STAY GUIDE

Host: **Romy and Howard**

Property: Your home in fun, thriving Causeway Bay, Hong Kong

Reference: Airbnb listing 15509244

Romy and Howard are Airbnb Superhosts with a Causeway Bay apartment in the heart of downtown Hong Kong. Shopping, restaurants and cinemas are at their guests' fingertips. Taxis, buses, trams and the MTR underground train are only steps away from their traditional 1950s 15-storey building. Victoria Park, Times Square and Hysan Place, Fashion Walk and Food Street are around the corner.

As long-term residents of Hong Kong, Romy and Howard rent out a bedroom and bathroom in the apartment they live in, and are on hand to answer any questions their guests might have about Hong Kong activities. They have a live-in domestic helper who keeps the apartment immaculate and cooks wonderful Asian, Middle Eastern and Moroccan food. Romy and Howard have been homeshare hosts for one year, but have had many friends and family from around the world staying with them. Most of their guests are young and are from other parts of Asia, staying in Hong Kong for a holiday or for a work trip; the guests love the apartment's location, which makes up for its relatively small size.

The most satisfying aspect of being a host:

The money we earn from homeshare helps to cover our rent. And we have met some lovely people from around the region, eager to hear our recommendations on Hong Kong.

A word of advice to new hosts:

Make sure you welcome your guests in person. It's the chance to get to know them, explain your house rules and answer any questions they have.

Host: **Megan and Sacha**

Property: Flora House – Downstairs Level, Seattle, United States

Reference: Airbnb listing 13913655

Megan and Sacha are Airbnb Superhosts whose homeshare is the recently renovated downstairs section of the house where they live with their two children.

The space for guests has two bedrooms and can sleep five people, with its own kitchen, bathroom and living area, as well as a separate entrance through the garden. Their home is close to Seattle airport, in a quiet, creative neighbourhood which tourists may not normally chose to visit. Megan and Sacha have been homeshare hosts for one year, but previously had long-term tenants in the downstairs section of their house. They celebrate the diversity of their guests and make sure to welcome them personally.

The most satisfying aspect of being a host:

We don't get to travel much ourselves, so this is a good way of connecting with the world. Especially in today's climate, it feels good to be welcoming strangers.

A word of advice to new hosts:

Avoid a rocky start. Do your research, talk to other hosts to avoid their pitfalls, learn what guests like before you start hosting. The more work you do up front, the better the guest experience will be and you will get good reviews straight away.

Host: **Sue**

Property: Kensington Apartment, London, United Kingdom

Reference: Airbnb listing 6018687

Sue is the owner of a three-bedroom apartment in Kensington, London, which is rented out for short-term visits. The apartment is managed by an Airbnb Superhost who looks after three homeshare properties. Sue's homeshare is only one block away from Holland Road and overlooks communal gardens; it is on the second floor of a Victorian terraced house and is perfect for visitors to Olympia shows or events, which are just a few minutes' walk away.

Sue has been a homeshare host for four years and initially listed with OneFineStay. More recently she has listed her apartment with Airbnb and VRBO too.

The most satisfying aspect of being a host:

Homesharing provides an additional source of revenue and outsourcing the associated work to a manager means that it is very easy for us.

A word of advice to new hosts:

Think through the logistics carefully, especially the cleaning and laundry between shares.

Host: **Tom and Britt**

Property: Kuća Kelsey, The Pearl of Povlja, Brač, Croatia and apartment
             in Stockholm, Sweden

Reference: kucakelsey.com

Tom and Britt are homeshare hosts whose Croatia property is a lovingly restored three-storey stone house with an olive grove for picnics. The house was built by a sea captain and is about 150 years old with its own two-storey wine cellar. While they have been careful not to disturb the original exterior of the building, the interior has all mod cons. The home-share can accommodate six people in its three bedrooms and two bathrooms; there is a fully equipped kitchen with stone countertops and a wood stove. A kayak is located on the waterfront for guest use. Brač is a beautiful island located a short ferry ride from Split and their little village is a great place for families to swim, hike and relax.

Tom and Britt started renting out their house in Croatia two years ago, during the summer season. This was their only rental property but, given the strong demand for temporary lodging in Stockholm, their other place of residence, they now also rent out their apartment there during spring and autumn. The demand for short-term rentals in Stockholm is so great that to advertise their apartment, they merely place an advertisement in the paper when they want to rent it.

The most satisfying aspect of being a host:

We like to support our village and hear back from the cafés and restaurants with their appreciation for us referring our guests.

A word of advice to new hosts:

Anticipate all eventualities and be prepared with information, resources and on-site staff. We spent a lot of time preparing a detailed house manual covering everything from the location of the fuse box, WiFi trouble-shooting, appliance instructions, to information on tourist attractions, ferry schedules, ATMs, car rentals, etc.

161

Host: **James**

Property: Tullamore, Blackheath, Blue Mountains, Australia

Reference: tullamoreblackheath.com/ or Airbnb listing 175407

James is an Airbnb Superhost whose homeshare is a 113-year-old cottage in the Blue Mountains, outside Sydney. The two-bedroom home has been renovated and retains original period features blended with comfortable contemporary furnishings and artworks. The modern country-styled kitchen has an adjoining dining room and a sunroom overlooking the beautiful gardens. Many of his guests come back regularly, some as often as four times per year.

James has been a host for nine years. He lives in a house opposite his homeshare, so he is available to guests if they need assistance.

The most satisfying aspect of being a host:

The money I earn from homeshare covers my mortgage and I also get to meet interesting people; it's a win-win.

A word of advice to new hosts:

Expect it to be busier than you think. Even in the beginning, hosting took more time than I expected. Think through the administration side carefully: there's a lot more to it than it seems, for example organizing insurance.

Host: **Ricci and Judy**

Properties: Apartments in Kuala Lumpur in Malaysia and Hong Kong

Reference: Airbnb listings 5290671 and 13336378

Ricci and Judy are homeshare hosts with two properties. Their three-bedroom apartment in Kuala Lumpur, Malaysia's capital city, is situated in a new apartment building with a gym. Their spacious, recently renovated two-bedroom apartment in Hong Kong has great harbour, park, city and mountain views and is one of the most booked and positively reviewed on TripAdvisor for Hong Kong; it sleeps up to eight guests. It is located in Causeway Bay, the heart of Hong Kong, is close to transport, and is a good place from which to watch fireworks or the nightly light show on the buildings of Kowloon.

   Ricci and Judy love to meet their guests and give them travel advice. They have been hosts for over five years; Ricci left his job to focus on homeshare and ensuring that his guests have a great experience. They use four online travel agents to market their homeshares: Airbnb, VRBO, Booking.com and TripAdvisor Vacation Rentals.

The most satisfying aspect of being a host:

Right now the money we earn from hosting is our main income, but the real satisfaction comes from meeting and helping visitors discover and explore our city.

A word of advice to new hosts:

The guest is king! Take care of them well and they will take care of you in the form of great reviews which are invaluable for attracting new guests.

Host: **Ingrid**

Property: The Vermont Escape, Whitingham, United States

Reference: Airbnb listing 4104708

Ingrid is an Airbnb Superhost whose homeshare is a two-bedroom apartment in her own home. The apartment is self-contained and has beautiful mountain views, just 20 minutes away from Mount Snow and a short walk to a lake where guests can swim in the summertime. Most guests are escaping the city for a break and enjoy the quiet, the mountain air and watching the stars at night.

Ingrid has been a host for three years and her homeshare is available from April to November each year. During the winter months, she works with disabled people on the ski fields.

The most satisfying aspect of being a host:

I enjoy meeting new people. I get satisfaction from seeing my guests in the garden enjoying the view, relaxing and taking a break.

A word of advice to new hosts:

Be there to welcome your guests. I always spend half an hour with my guests when they arrive, show them everything in the apartment and make sure that they understand my house rules.

Host: **Helen**

Property: Terrace house, Paddington, Sydney, Australia

Reference: Airbnb listing 1886465

Helen offers her home for homeshare when she travels, typically for a couple of months each year. Her bijou sunny modern two-bedroom terraced house with parking is hidden away in a tiny mews behind Sydney's trendy Oxford Street, Paddington. The house is just seconds away from the many designer shops, galleries, restaurants and bars; peaceful, yet in the midst of it all.

Helen's guests are never the same: she has had a few longer-stay corporate bookings, mature couples on world trips, and even a concert pianist on tour. Helen has been a host for four years.

The most satisfying aspect of being a host:

The income I receive from sharing my home covers the expenses of my overseas travel when I am away.

A word of advice to new hosts:

Homesharing is a great way to supplement your income but like all things, requires effort to be successful.

Host: **Derrick**

Property: Sunset Pavilions and Choengmon Gardens, Koh Samui, Thailand

Reference: samuisunsetpavilions.com and choengmongardens.com

Derrick is the homeshare host for two properties on Koh Samui island in Thailand. Sunset Pavilions is a spacious villa with four-bedroom suites, a swimming pool, full kitchen and sauna. Guests can enjoy sea views and local staff can assist with catering and sightseeing if required. The Choengmon Gardens resort consists of two- and three-bedroom town houses for guests.

Derrick has been a part-time host for ten years and a full-time host for five years.

The most satisfying aspect of being a host:

Homesharing is a great way to earn a living while living in a wonderful place.

A word of advice to new hosts:

It is of prime importance to have your own website to maintain control of your own business and have personal contact with your prospective and past clients.

Host: **Yvonne and Paul**

Property: Chateau and Groom's Cottage in Bouresse, France and
             Darlinghurst apartment in Sydney, Australia

Reference: Airbnb listings 13021846, 12857999 and 5375483

Yvonne and Paul are Airbnb Superhosts whose homeshare properties are
in rural France and Sydney, Australia. In France, their guests enjoy a
recently renovated nine-bedroom castle set in 2.5 hectares of beautiful
gardens, with a swimming pool, sauna and wine cellar. The groom's
cottage is also available for rentals. During the winter, guests can experience boar hunting at the neighbouring chateau.

  Their Australian apartment is their primary home and is located in
central Sydney. A well-known Australian interior designer renovated it and
when they are away, they rent it out. Its location is close to restaurants,
galleries, cinemas, transport and the city is ideal for visitors to Sydney.

  Yvonne and Paul have been hosts for 25 years, originally running homeshares in rural Australia. They are passionate restorers of old buildings and
instead of retiring, they bought a castle to renovate and operate as a
homeshare. They were early adopters of Airbnb when it first started in
Australia six years ago.

The most satisfying aspect of being a host:

*Being a homesharing host is wonderful because one meets people
from all walks of life, and there are simultaneous financial returns.*

A word of advice to new hosts:

*Don't underestimate the demands on you as a host. It's no good
being a host if you don't want to clean up after your guests; you
need to have hospitality in your blood.*

Host: **Sidharth**

Property: Nirvana Villa, Infinity Villas in Lonavala, India

Reference: Airbnb listing 12117671

Sidharth is a host whose homeshare is a villa located in Lonavala, a small city approximately 100 kilometres from Mumbai. The four-bedroom house is only a five-minute drive from the marketplace, but it feels secluded, nestled into the base of a small mountain which is beautifully green during the monsoon season. The villa has a garden and swimming pool, and a local chef who is available to cook for guests.

Sidharth has been a host for two years and is committed to contributing to his community by providing employment opportunities and promoting local products. He previously worked in real estate and property development and now also manages the homeshare properties for another 15 local hosts.

The most satisfying aspect of being a host:

I get satisfaction from providing jobs and from promoting local produce at my homeshare.

A word of advice to new hosts:

When you are starting out, don't be too rigid on pricing. Be flexible, begin with low nightly rates to attract lots of bookings, make sure you get good reviews to build a sense of trust for future guests, and then you can put your prices up.

Host: **Brianna and Mitch**

Property: Bondi studio apartment, Sydney and apartment in Kingscliff,
             Australia

Reference: Airbnb listings 5739875 and 9189046

Brianna and Mitch are Airbnb Superhosts with two homeshare properties. Their studio apartment at Sydney's Bondi, within walking distance of the famous beach, is a cosy apartment with views of the coastline.

Their second homeshare is a two-bedroom apartment with ocean views, a new kitchen and a balcony in a town in northern New South Wales. This apartment is part of the five-star Bale resort, so guest can use the resort facilities during their visit, including swimming pools, spa, BBQs, tennis court, gym and bars.

Brianna and Mitch have been hosting for three years.

The most satisfying aspect of being a host:

I love knowing that we've thought of everything that our guests would like, right down to the toys for the beach.

A word of advice to new hosts:

Reduce your workload by anticipating what your guests will ask. Leave clear instructions for your guests (such as the WiFi password) to minimize the number of times they contact you.

Host: **Ray**

Property: Luxury Rental Dublin, Lower Mount Street, Dublin, Ireland

Reference: Airbnb listing 13396305 and luxuryrentaldublin.com

Ray is the homeshare host for a two-bedroom apartment in central Dublin, just a five-minute walk from Trinity College. Ray manages 23 properties in Dublin which are available for short-term lets; they are all inspected and curated by his staff. His team is responsible for sales and marketing, the preparation of the properties and transitions between guests, as well as the guest experience. They are only a phone call away to answer guest questions during their visit. Ray's guests typically collect their keys from the Luxury Rental Dublin downtown office where staff greet them with the traditional Irish welcome of 'Céad míle fáilte!'

Ray has been managing homeshares as a commercial operator for two years.

The most satisfying aspect of being a host:

It is satisfying to know that through our attention to detail, our guests to Dublin have a wonderful experience here.

A word of advice to new hosts:

Always focus on the customer and pay attention to every detail – down to the smallest item.

Host: **Isaiah**

Property: 5-Star Quiet, Central Luxury Apartment, San Diego, United States

Reference: Airbnb listing 2463167

Isaiah is an Airbnb Superhost whose homeshare is his apartment in the heart of San Diego. He lives in one bedroom and rents out the other bedroom using various online travel agencies, including Airbnb and MisterB&B. The apartment is less than a 10-minute drive to most attractions in San Diego, and only 15 minutes to the beach; Balboa Park and the San Diego Zoo are a short walk away. The complex has been renovated and has a beautiful courtyard with a covered cabana area for lounging and relaxing. Isaiah enjoys interacting with his guests and helping make their stay in San Diego memorable.

Isaiah has been a homeshare host for three years. He intends to purchase another property so he can rent out the entire apartment, as well as renting out a room in his new home.

The most satisfying aspect of being a host:

The best thing about hosting is the flexibility I maintain with my home. If I have friends or family coming to town, I can block off my calendar and let them stay with me so they don't have to pay for a hotel. If I just want to have my home to myself for a few days, I have that flexibility as well.

A word of advice to new hosts:

Treat your home like your guest is about to stay in a hotel – keep it clean and tidy. Your reviews will reflect this and in turn, bring more guests to your home. And remember that first impressions are everything. Kerb appeal is the start of a guest's impression, so make sure your home is on-point at all times!

B. HOMESHARE SOLUTIONS

The experiences we have shared in this book are complemented by HomeShare Solutions, an online service that we run for homeshare hosts around the world.

The HomeShare Solutions Vision
- To provide hosts with the confidence to run successful homeshare businesses
- To establish an online community where homeshare hosts can share information and best practices
- To improve the quality of homeshare accommodation so as to enhance the guest experience

HomeShare Solutions aims to provide homeshare hosts with:
- Basic training and advice on how to run a homeshare business.
- The tools, checklists, financial models and scorecards to support their homeshare business.
- An online community of homeshare hosts where hosts can ask questions and share information with other hosts.
- Case studies and stories from other hosts.
- Benchmark data.
- Webinars and one-on-one consulting advice.

HomeShare Solutions is structured in the same way as this book. Information is provided in the form of diagrams, tools, checklists, short instructional videos, frequently asked questions, webinars and TED-like talks on hot topics.

Case study videos bring to life the realities of homeshare

hosting. Hosts tell their stories – what has worked well for them, what challenges they have encountered and how they resolved problems. They share the lessons they have learned along the way.

There is also a place for you to post your comments about this book and to discuss what you have learned about home-sharing with other hosts.

Please visit www.homesharesolutions.com to find out more.

C. REFERENCE MATERIAL

The homeshare industry is growing fast and every day more resources are made available for hosts. The information offered to subscribers by online travel agents is definitely worth consulting, as is some literature from the hospitality industry. At the time of publishing, the authors had found the following useful, independent information for homeshare hosts.

Afford Anything blog by Paula Pant
Presents financial projections including her homeshare experience
affordanything.com/blog/

AirDNA, Airbnb Data and Analytics
Provides statistics on Airbnb properties, with access to The Airbnb Expert's Playbook, Secrets to Making six-Digits as a Rentalpreneur, by Scott Shatford
blog.airdna.co/

BnbStaging Le Blog, by Katia, an interior designer in Paris
Tips on hospitality and housekeeping for Airbnb hosts
en.blog.bnbstaging.com/

GetProperly
An app to manage transitions, recommended by Airbnb
www.getproperly.com/en

Little Hotelier
Advice for small hotels (which can be applicable to homeshares)
littlehotelier.com/calculate-your-occupancy-rate/

Lynda training course: Making Money with Airbnb
With Charles Matthew Spencer
lynda.com/AirBnB-tutorials/Making-Money-
  AirBnB/385691-2.html

Peak: How Great Companies Get Their Mojo from Maslo
By Chip Conley
chipconley.com/writing/

The Perfect Stay
Curated by Daniel Kerzner
theperfectstay.com/

Our Keys, Your Home
The Senior Nomads, Michael and Debbie Campbell
  Blog and book advice from experienced Airbnb guests
  for hosts
seniornomads.com/blog/

Acknowledgements

We would like to acknowledge the contributions of many people who have not only made this book possible, but also helped to enhance the Dantosa guest experience. A big thank you goes to our fellow homeshare hosts who willingly shared their experiences and advice, and to our colleagues:

- Liana Cafolla, who embraced this project enthusiastically and worked to a very aggressive deadline
- Geoff Turner, for giving us the language to discuss our home-share business, and the hospitality experience to make sense of it
- Romy Serfaty, whose enthusiasm and advice has been continuous during this project
- Chris Kyme, whose creative vision elevated the marketing for Dantosa
- Bernice Rossouw, whose talent as a designer is setting new homeshare benchmarks.

Thanks to the following people for their hard work at Dantosa:

- Derek Pracey, whose remarkable expertise ensures that Dantosa's gardens are always presentable for our guests
- Alex King, who is always happy to be called on for maintenance and building at Dantosa

- David, Peter and Brian Young, whose hard work and cheerful assistance with our Sydney apartment has been invaluable
- Ann and Michael Begg, who supported us in the first stage of our homeshare journey.

And to the people who helped with the writing and review of this book:

- Joan Domicelj for happily reading and reviewing our draft at short notice and for her optimistic support for this project
- Michael Sylvester, who reviewed content as a prospective host, challenged our thinking and hosted us in Los Angeles
- Tamara Domicelj, Judith Brine and Joan Domicelj for brainstorming on suitable names for our initial book, *The HomeShare Journey*
- The guests who have stayed at Dantosa, whose support and feedback has made this homeshare journey possible
- The Airbnb founders and community who have provided forums and avenues to continue to challenge our assumptions about hosting and to motivate us to continuously strive to do better.

And most importantly, our immediate and extended families, who deliver constant encouragement and assistance to us.

Index